LANCASHIRE

WATERSIDE WALKS

RAY KNAPMAN

ISBN 9798596871883

Photographs : Ray Knapman unless otherwise stated
Maps : Drawn by Ray Knapman and based on Open street map.
Cover Photographs : Front cover : Newton Bridge on the River Hodder;
   Back Cover : The weir at Abbeystead

Disclaimer : The information given in this book is for guidance at the time
   of publication. It is recommended that OS maps are used for navigation
   on the walks. It is only the individual that can determine their ability,
   fitness, experience and competence for their own safety on the walks.

Walk location map showing significant rivers and roads

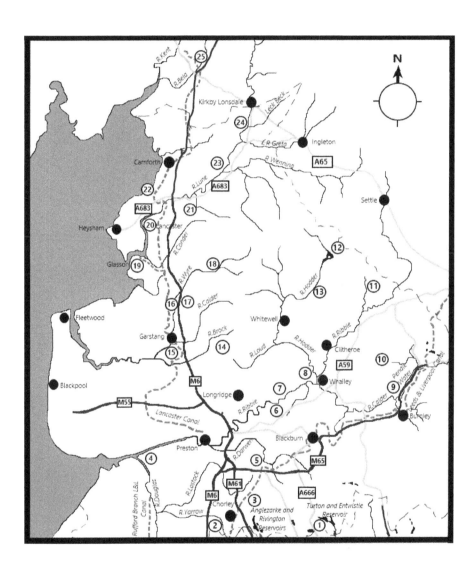

CONTENTS

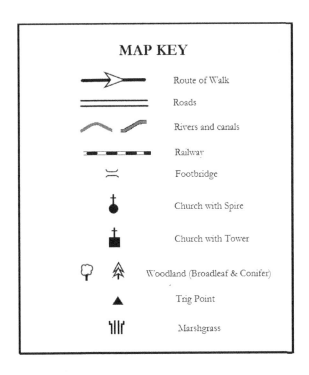

INTRODUCTION

Lancashire's rivers and canals flow through beautiful scenery that rivals the very best to be found in England. In this book I have gathered together 25 outstanding circular walks, each of which follows the course of a river, canal or the Lancashire shoreline.

Lancashire has a great variety of landscapes, from the low rounded hills of the Forest of Bowland and Pendle Hill intersected by the valleys of the rivers Lune, Wyre, Ribble, Hodder, and Calder, to the flat coastal landscape and salt marshes to be found along the banks of the Ribble estuary and River Douglas. Special mention is given to the valley of the River Hodder, for it is acclaimed as the most beautiful in England , rumoured to be endorsed by no less than the Queen who has intimated she would retire here if she could!

Waterside paths add interest and character to a walk, with stone bridges, stepping stones, weirs, and the variable nature of the water courses through the seasons, and a greater variety of plant and bird life. Besides the usual ducks and geese, birds such as Dipper, Heron, Wagtail, Egret, Curlew , Oystercatcher and Kingfisher may be seen along many of the waterways of Lancashire. The chosen routes explore the courses of the waterways, adding an extra dimension for an enjoyable walking experience. They include notable antiquities such as ancient pack horse bridges, Roman forts, Stoneyhurst College of J.R. Tolkien fame, the small working harbour at Glasson Dock, and the Lancaster Canal.

All the walks may be accessed from either the M6 or M65/A65 corridors, making the starting points within an hour's drive from the Manchester and Merseyside conurbations. Lancashire has some great walks and interest here on our doorstep, and are easily accessible when a quick decision is made to take advantage of a spell of fair weather for a local walk.

For each of the walks, points of interest are indicated, including noteworthy historical places, and places for refreshment. Information is given to get to the starting point including the postcode. Photos and notes on what to look out for are provided to add interest to the walk, most may be achieved by an average fit person.

Walk Categories

I have classified the walks into 3 categories: -

Easy	5 to 6 miles on fairly flat ground.
Moderate	6 to 9 miles with some short climbs
Hard	over 9 Miles

Most of the walks are on well-defined paths near to shelter. Some walks do necessitate walking on tarmac but this has been kept to a minimum. Although most of the walks are close to shelter and sustenance, all walking should be undertaken with appropriate walking shoes/boots and protective rainwear. On all the walks muddy conditions may be encountered and should be prepared for. Young children and dogs must be closely supervised especially near railway lines and canals, and where there are farm animals.

I have purposely omitted an estimated time for each walk as there is a huge difference in people's outlook on walking ,some like to ponder and absorb as they go, and the opposite extreme for some walkers is to do a walk as energetically as possible. There are of course other factors such as ability and stamina to consider, but if an estimate is required, a rule of thumb guide for the average walker I have found a rate of 2 mile an hour is a fair estimation.

It is strongly advisable to use Ordnance Survey maps and not rely on the sketch maps for navigation. Maps used are OS 1:25000 Explorer for their more detailed interpretation of ground features and elevation. But for most walks the OS 1:50000 Landranger series are more than adequate. These are :- 102 Preston, Blackpool; 103 Blackburn & Burnley; 97 Kendal & Morecambe

Acknowledgements.

Many thanks to all my friends in the BT Walking club whose walks have been invaluable in providing ideas and inspiration for the book.

WALK 1

Wayoh, Turton and Entwistle Reservoirs

A pleasant level walk round the reservoirs which nestle in the folds of the hills of Turton Moor north of Bolton.

ROUTE SUMMARY	Wayoh Reservoir – Turton Reservoir – Entwistle Station – Turton Bottoms – Jumble Reservoir - Chapeltown
START	Embankment Road, Chapeltown
LOCATION & ATTRIBUTES	
Distance and Grading	7 ¼ Miles 740 Feet (225 Mts)ascent Moderate
Route conditions	Mostly good well used paths ,few inclines and a little road side walking and no stiles
Postcode	BL7 0NA
Grid Reference	SD733161
Refreshments	Strawbury Duck pub , half way round in Entwistle
Car parking	Roadside parking on Embankment Road
Toilets	At the pub

Directions to the walk

From the M6 /M61 join the M65. Leave the M65 at junction 4 onto the A666 towards Darwen then continue on through Darwen for 2 ½ miles, turn left onto B 6391 . Follow towards Chapeltown ,look out for left turning onto Embankment Road after the Chapeltown boundary sign.

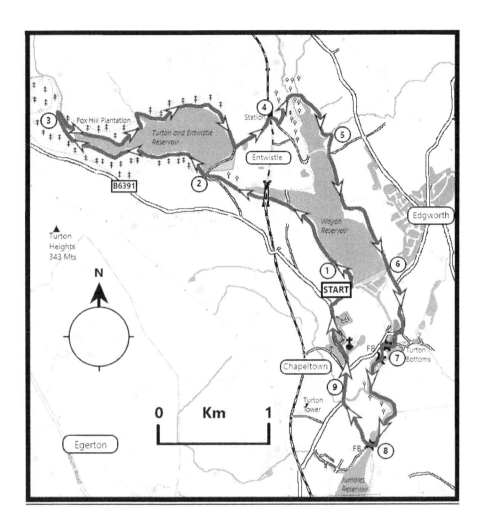

Walk Description

The walk follows paths around the two reservoirs of Turton and Entwistle and Wayoh. The paths are level and are great for viewing the wild fowl and other abundant birdlife in the area. The hills of Turton Moor shelter the valley in which the reservoirs where built for thewater catchment of the many brooks including the Bradshaw Brook, that flow into it. Starting from the village of Chapeltown the route quickly drops down to the path that skirts the Wayoh Reservoir before passing under the impressive Armsgrove Viaduct which carries the Bolton to Blackburn railway high above an arm of the reservoir.The route then climbs to reach the largest reservoir of the group ; the Turton and Entwistle and follows the broad path up to its head at Yarnside.

The path crosses many footbridges over the brooks that feed it and skirts the reservoir back to reach the dam. A short stretch of track leads to the incongruous sight of a pub, the improbably named "Strawbury Duck" seemingly in

View from footbridge over the brook at Yarnside

the middle of nowhere, it has refreshments and atmosphere so well worth a drop in.

Next to the pub is a railway station, Entwistle, which by the way is a good alternative way of doing this walk by catching a train from Bolton and finishing at the pub. The station is a novelty as it is a request stop, the trains only stop by a hand signal or request to the conductor.

The route continues by following the path down to another arm of the Wayoh Reservoir and following the waterside path which passes information boards containing identification of the various birdlife to be found in the area.

The path leaves the reservoir at the dam and drops down to the village of Edgeworth and The Black Bull pub ,a short stretch of roadside walking leads through a pretty stretch through housing with cobblestone drives and colourful gardens, with the Bradshaw Brook babbling its way under arched stone bridges.

This brook is then followed on a delightful stretch as it winds its way into the Wayoh Reservoir through what appears to be a mini gorge. A footbridge is crossed to reach a path which leads on to the road through Chapeltown and the distinctive elegant church spire of St Annes. A short walk along the High Street leads on to the cul de sac at the Embankment .This is a good all season walk with good level paths ,no stiles and no steep inclines.

Walk Directions

1. Follow the path from the road to reach the dam, and turn left on the path alongside the reservoir. Pass the causeway and under the railway viaduct. Climb the path to reach a car park below the Turton and Entwistle Dam.

2. Pass through the car park onto the road across the dam, then bear left to follow the reservoir path. Continue on up to the headwaters of the dam at Foxhill Plantation.

3. Cross the footbridge over Cadshaw Brook and bear right, continue to follow the reservoir path. Cross a footbridge at Simms Clough , continue on the path to the dam. Climb up to the road over the dam and turn left to follow the road.

4. At the Strawbury Duck (a great place for a break!) carry on to pass over the railway bridge. Bear right and in a few Mts ,turn left through a gate . Follow the steep descending path, stay on the path to pass over two footbridges and turn right onto the path alongside the Wayoh Rreservoir.

5. Cross a footbridge over an inlet . then cross a road on a curved causeway. Continue to follow the path alongside the reservoir to reach the dam.

The Strawbury Duck

6. Leave the reservoir path and drop down to the road at the Black Bull pub in Edgeworth. Turn right downhill and follow the road. After 250 Mts. turn left onto Birches Road and in a few Mts. bear right at a fork.

7. Turn right to cross a narrow bridge over Bradshaw Brook, then turn left and follow the street to another bridge over Bradshaw Brook. Cross the bridge and turn right to follow the brookside path through a mini gorge down to the headwaters of Jumbles Reservoir

The path alongside Bradshaw Brook to Jumbles reservoir

8. Cross a footbridge over an inlet and follow the path uphill bearing right. Pass a pill box and continue up to a junction with Chapeltown Road.

9. Turn right and follow the road past St Annes Church with its fine looking spire and continue along the High Street to reach the Embankment Road.

WALK 2

Charnock Green and the River Yarrow

A level walk with riverside paths, woodland and farmland scenery, interest and variety in all seasons

ROUTE SUMMARY	Charnock Green – Pincock – Bradley Hall – Heskin Green – Park Hall
START	The Bowling Green pub at Charnock Richard
LOCATION & ATTRIBUTES	
Distance and Grading	6 ¾ Miles – 347 Feet (106 Mts.) ascent - Moderate
Route conditions	Mostly on good level paths and tracks but some muddy conditions to be expected. A few stiles and some quiet road walking
Postcode	PR7 5LA
Grid Reference	SD 553168
Refreshments	Bowling Green pub on the A49
Car parking	As above
Toilets	As above

Directions to the walk

Leave the M6 at junction27, follow the A 5209 toward Standish, turn left at the lights in Standish onto the A46, follow 4/5 miles through Charnock Richard, the Bowling Green pub is on the left.

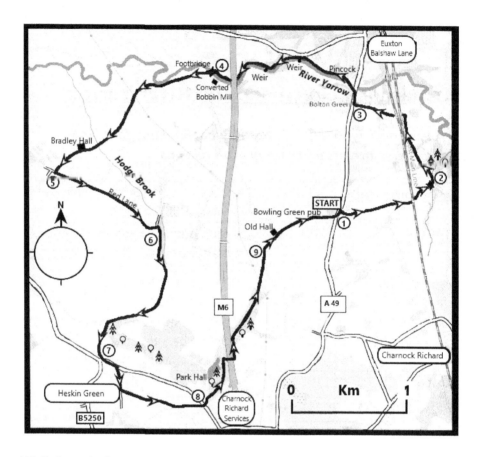

Walk Description

   The walk follows paths through a variety of surprisingly rural landscapes considering how close you are to Chorley town centre. The stretch alongside the River Yarrow is particularly beautiful in late spring. There are a couple of weirs on the route which can be spectacular following a rainy spell. The paths follow the wooded fringes of flat expansive farmland, quiet lanes and the large Park Hall estate. Start at the Bowling Green Inn where a great variety of food and drink may be had at the end of your walk, I think this makes for a great winter walk not too long or arduous and a finish at the pub in a nice warm friendly atmosphere.

The weir on the River Yarrow at Pincock

Walk Directions

1. Cross the A49 then follow Delph Lane opposite a few metres and turn left onto a path alongside a boundary hedge. Cross the footbridge over the West Coast Main Railway Line and continue on path to a stile and footbridge cross and turn left to follow the lane metalled road (German Lane) and turn left.

2. Follow the lane down to pass under a double railway bridge. Carry on to the A49.

3. Turn right on the main road, cross carefully and in a few Mts., turn left before a bridge over the River Yarrow onto Pincock Brow. Follow the road over the narrow bridge over the river and turn left onto Pincock Street. At the end of the street,

Pincock Bridge and water guage

15

continue to follow the riverside path, passing under the M6. Join a track, (Mill Lane) follow it to reach grand looking Bobbin Mill conversion on the bank of the river.

Bobbin Mill and the River Yarrow

4. Cross a footbridge directly after the house, bear right onto a path alongside field boundary, then cross a field path to a path junction. Bear left continue to follow the field boundary cross a footbridge and under a transmission line. Carry on past a small pond to a gate, bear right on a faint field path to reach Bradley Hall Farm, cross Hodge Brook and follow the access track to Red Lane.

5. Turn left, follow the lane 600 Mts. to a sharp left bend. Shortly after look out for a way marked path on your right.

6. Turn right to follow the path past a small pond. Continue along the tree lined path beside Hodge Brook. At a junction of paths continue straight on to cross a footbridge and onto Park Hall Road.

7. Turn left, a few Mt's on turn right onto Stocks Lane. In a 150 Mt's turn left onto waymarked path just past Stocks Court. Cross a footbridge and bear left on field path uphill to reach Park Hall Road at a gate and stile.

8. Cross carefully and follow the drive opposite, then bear right following the drive, turn right onto a path to reach a footbridge over the M6. After the bridge, follow the path and track to reach Old Hall Lane.

9. Follow the lane which brings you back to the A49 and the Bowling Green pub.

WALK 3

Wheelton to White Coppice

A walk of great variety, with hamlets, open pasturelands, and woodlands, following paths alongside streams, reservoirs and a canal towpath through rural countryside.

ROUTE SUMMARY	Wheelton –Leeds Liverpool Canal - Brinscall – White Coppice – Heapey Reservoirs - Johnsons Hillock Locks
START	Top Lock pub at Wheelton

LOCATION & ATTRIBUTES	
Distance and Grading	7 ¼ Miles 600Feet (183Mt's) ascent moderate
Route conditions	The route follows mainly well marked paths and tracks, there are some field paths and mainly quiet roadside walking, quite a few stiles but no steep gradients
Postcode	PR6 8LP
Grid Reference	SD 596214
Refreshments	At The Top Lock pub and café at White Coppice
Car parking	As above; limited street parking near the pub
Toilets	As above

Directions to the walk

Leave the M61 at junction 8, follow the A674 toward Blackburn after 1 ½ miles turn left for Whittle le Woods, at a mini roundabout take the second exit. Turn right onto Dark Lane just before a canal bridge ,follow to a T junction ,turn right then left

18

onto Copthurst Lane. The Top Lock car park is on the left just before a canal bridge.

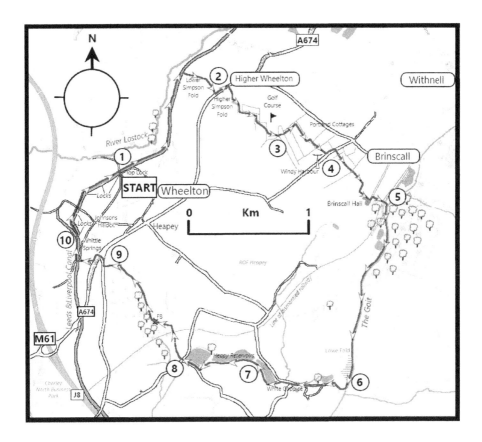

Walk Description

From the Top Lock the walk sets off along a stretch of the Leeds Liverpool Canal, where many canal boats are moored along both banks .Soon the canal passes through a tree lined stretch and the scenery becomes very rural. There are nice countryside views along the towpath and a wealth of wildlife can be seen, birds, waterfowl and ducks abound. The River Lostock flows on your left in a gulley marked by the trees of Denham Wood, soon after the route leaves the canal and passes through the hamlet of Higher Wheelton where paths are followed across a patchwork of fields to reach Windy Harbour marked by a tall telecommunications mast.

Following on from here the route descends on a field path to reach Brinscall Hall, at the edge of the West Pennine Moors. A little further on the route passes under a bridge on the line of a dismantled railway before joining The Goit, a channel built to tap into the reservoirs at Roddlesworth to supplement the water supply of the Rivington Reservoirs.

The route follows the channel through quite dense woodland to reach White Coppice, a picturesque spot with a cricket ground with stone cottages and a café, overlooked by hills on all sides. This is a popular visitor spot and can get crowded on warm summer weekends but if the café is open this is a good place for a refreshment break.

Continuing on through the hamlet the road follows a stream, in springtime there is a wonderful display of flowers which deck the banking alongside the road. Further on the route follows a path along a succession of small reservoirs, the route then passes under the dismantled railway again. The line closed in the 60's and linked Chorley with Blackburn. Shortly after the track leads on through woodland to reach the A674 which is quickly crossed and onto the sanctuary of the towpath of the Leeds & Liverpool Canal. The towpath is followed to the engineering marvel of the four staircase Johnson's Hillock Locks and pounds which together with the three subsequent locks gives a rise of 66

The Top Lock Pub

feet to the canal. A short branch at the foot of the staircase was intended to link with the Lancaster Canal at Preston, but this proved to be too expensive so the branch was terminated at a basin at Walton Summit. The Top Lock pub, as its name suggests is at the end of the series of locks and is a fitting end to the walk with a typical canal side atmosphere, great food and refreshments.

Walk Directions

1. From the pub car park ,cross the canal bridge and turn right to follow the road past the lock and onto the tow path, follow the path to reach bridge number 85 Simpsons Fold Bridge. Leave the towpath ,cross the bridge and follow the track onto the A 674.

2. Turn left, follow the road100Mts. and turn right onto Fishwick Lane. Turn left past a private house ,follow the right field boundary under a power line. Cross a farm track and continue to a line of trees. Bear left, follow the line of trees, cross a stile and continue along the boundary on your left. Cross a stile and turn right along the boundary on your right, then after passing between a line of trees ,bear left to follow the tree line. Cut across a field corner to reach the boundary of the golf course and turn right ,follow the boundary to a footbridge ,cross and continue along the boundary of the golf course now on your right.

3. At a junction of paths at a field crossing , carry straight on across the field to the opposite boundary, cross and continue along the left boundary over two fields , then turn right alongside the next boundary. Head for the transmission mast seen ahead. Cross a stile ,the boundary turns left and right ,cross another stile then follow the field boundary on your right, cross the boundary by two trees and follow the fenceline to reach a paddock and a stile onto Harbour Lane.

4. Turn left ,follow the road 50 Mts ,turn right to cross a stile onto a field path, follow the left boundary fence, cross a stile and continue on down bearing right towards a tree lined road. Turn left on the road(Briars Brow) continue on past the impressive Brinscall Hall Turn left onto Dicks Lane ,in a few Mts ,turn right onto a track, pass under the arched bridge beneath dismantled railway line and shortly after, cross a drive.

5. Turn right on a broad track alongside The Goit. The track follows the water course all the way to White Coppice through dense woodland .After crossing a few tracks with gates you reach a major crossing at a cricket

The path along the Goit

pitch at White Coppice, where there may be a chance for refreshment.and stop awhile and soak in the ambience of this special location

Springtime at White Coppice

6. Continue on the road past the cricket pitch to a junction, bear left, follow the road past a reservoir on the right and straight on at another junction past another reservoir on your left. Continue on passing a delightful scene of white terraced cottages and a ford through a brook on your right. The place is especially scenic in spring with daffodils all along the side of the road. After crossing the brook turn off at the waymarked path over a footbridge on the left. Follow the path around another reservoir to reach a track.

7. Cross the track and continue on the path opposite to follow another reservoir to reach a car park ,bear right on a path down to a lane and turn right At a T junction, carry straight on across the road onto a track.

8. Follow the track to pass under an arched dismantled railway bridge, shortly after bear left on a field path towards woodland. Cross a footbridge and continue through the wood alongside Tan House Brook. The wood thins out , and the path bends left towards housing. Continue to follow the path which ends in a ginnel through the housing onto Blackburn Road.

9. Turn right to the A 674, cross the dual carriageway at the junction and turn left on the path alongside the road to reach Moss Lane at a roundabout . Keep straight on the main road opposite(to the right of the Premier Inn)to reach the canal bridge .Cross and turn right back down to reach the tow path and turn left.

10. Follow the towpath to the staircase locks ,cross the footbridge over the truncated branch and follow the path alongside the locks and the pounds in between. Cross Town Lane and continue along the towpath to reach Top Lock pub.

WALK 4

Longton Marshlands of the River Douglas

An atmospheric walk alongside the tidal estuary of the River Douglas.

ROUTE SUMMARY	Longton – Pilot's Cottage - Ribble Way – The Dolphin – Little Hoole – Much Hoole – Odd House Farm
START	Longton Brickcroft Nature Reserve
LOCATION & ATTRIBUTES	

Distance and Grading	7 ¾ Miles 165 Feet (50 Mt's) ascent Easy
Route conditions	Mainly flat with a few stiles, some roadside walking, but mainly on remote paths and farm tracks.
Postcode	PR4 4SB
Grid Reference	SD 479251
Refreshments	The Dolphin on Marsh Lane
Car parking	Car park at Longton Brickcroft Nature Reserve
Toilets	At the reserve, check opening times

Directions to the walk

Leave the M6 at junction 29 (M61 at junction 9), onto the M65 then follow the A582 towards Leyland. At a pair of roundabouts, follow theA582 towards Preston. At the next large roundabout bear left to follow the B5253 towards Leyland, continue to the next roundabout and take the third exit for Longton. Follow on to another roundabout and take the third exit (Reiver Road). After ½

24

Mile turn right onto Midge Hall Lane. Follow to the A59, turn left, follow the road to a roundabout and take the fifth exit for Longton. The Brickcroft Nature Reserve is on the right

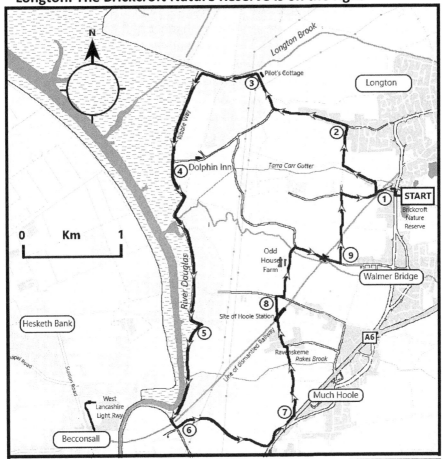

Walk Description

The walk starts from Longton Brickcroft, formerly a brickwork which has been transformed into a nature reserve and public open space. The site is extremely attractive for nature lovers with the former clay pits now filled with water and landscaped.

The atmospheric walk with open views akin to flat fenland scenery alongside the tidal estuary of the River Douglas, is also great for bird watchers as it is the natural home for a large variety of visiting and indigenous wildfowl.

The route mainly follows along the flood protection dykes which give wide reaching views over the flat landscape and saltmarshes. The marshlands are a large area lying at the confluence of the Rivers Douglas and Ribble. A short stretch of the 70 mile Ribble Way path is followed from the old Pilot House to its starting point at the Dolphin Inn.

The tidal River Douglas is followed up to a marina .At high tide canal boats sometimes use the river to make the perilous crossing from the Rufford Branch of the Leeds Liverpool Canal to the River Ribble and follow it upstream to reach locks for the Lancaster Canal.at Savick Brook.

The route continues on crossing an embankment for a dismantled railway and over patchwork of field paths to reach the site of the long gone Hoole railway station .Further on the bridge abutments for the railway are passed on Station Road. Further field paths and country lanes bring you back to the start at Brickcroft Nature Reserve.

Walk Directions

1. From the entrance turn right then left down Longton Hall Lane. Turn right down Meadow Head Lane. At the end of the lane turn left onto a track and follow to offset crossroads. Turn right follow the path past nurseries and through housing to reach Marsh Lane

2. Turn left to follow Marsh Lane 600 Mt's then turn right onto Grange Lane. Follow the lane to its end where the old converted Pilots Cottage stands.

The Pilot House

3. Turn left to follow a track leading on to join the Ribble Way. Follow the track on the dyke to reach a gate and stile at a waymarker.

4. Cross the stile and either continue on or turn left on the track which leads you to The Dolphin, 200 Mt's on for a comfort break. Continue along the dyke on to another stile and waymarker. Bear right before the stile and follow the dyke alongside the saltmarshes. The path turns left next a brook to reach a track.

5. Turn right to follow the track which follows the dyke alongside the river. At a crossroads, to view the marina and jetty on the river, turn right along the dyke. Return to the crossroads and continue straight on crossing the alignment of the dismantled West Lancashire Railway to reach a gate and stile on a tarmacked road

Longton Dyke

6. Turn left onto a farm track and follow the boundary between fields passing under two power transmission lines to reach the A59. Turn left, follow the road 200 Mts.

7. Turn left at a gap in the hedge onto a path alongside a boundary hedge and under a power line. Cross a footbridge, turn left then shortly right. Continue along the boundary on the left, cross a small bridge over Rakes Brook and bear left to reach the small hamlet at Ravenskerne . Turn left on the tarmacked road then right

Pylons on the flat landscape at Hoole

at the waymarked driveway past residential housing. Cross a field path straight on to another boundary hedge on a track.

8. This is the line of the dismantled railway at Hoole Station which was closed to all traffic in 1964. Cross the trackbed and onto a path directly opposite, follow a field path to reach a stile onto Station Road. Turn right,follow the road a few Mts. then turn left onto a track. Pass a waymarker showing the path bearing right past Odd House Farm, continue to reach Hall Carr Lane. Turn right, follow the road passing between the bridge abutments of the dismantled railway, look out for a waymarked path at a gate on the left next a pair of houses.

9. Turn left through the gate. Keep straight on alongside hedges and through gates then past a pond to reach Hall Lane. Turn right, follow the lane to the main road and the Brickcroft Nature Reserve opposite the junction.

WALK 5

Riley Green and Houghton Bottoms

A great local pub walk which circles the ancient Houghton Tower grounds. The varied route follows field paths, quiet country lanes, riverside and canal towpaths.

ROUTE SUMMARY	Riley Green – Hoghton Bottoms – River Darwen – Leeds and Liverpool Canal towpath
START	Royal Oak pub.

LOCATION & ATTRIBUTES	
Distance and Grading	4 ½ Miles - 490 Ft (149 Mt's) ascent - Easy
Route conditions	Mainly level paths, some can be muddy, a few stiles and one short steep stretch.
Postcode	PR5 0SJ
Grid Reference	SD622255
Refreshments	The Royal Oak at Riley Green; very good food and charming staff
Car parking	At the pub
Toilets	At the pub

Directions to the walk

Leave the M65 at junction 3, follow the A 675 toward Bolton, in less than a mile, turn right at Riley Green, the Royal Oak pub is a few yards on the left.

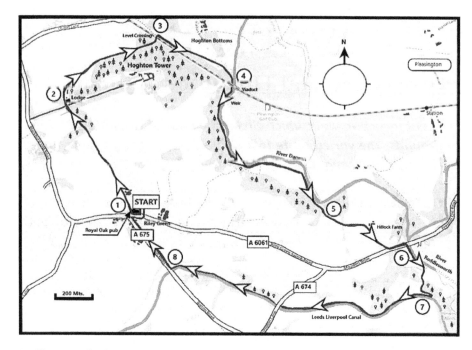

Walk Description

Starting at the Royal Oak, the route soon enters tranquil rural calming countryside which belies the proximity of the roaring M65. The route follows a path gently ascending open field paths to reach the grounds of Houghton Tower.

The drive up to Houghton Tower is crossed at a lodge house, in early spring there is a blanket of snowdrops beneath the woodland canopy. A woodland path takes you down to Houghton Bottoms with a tiny stone hamlet lies beneath the high railway viaduct over the River Darwen.

A riverside path follows the river past a weir which is at the top of a picturesque sandstone gorge. This local landmark is a part of local history as it once provided water mill power for Higher Mill and Livesey's Cotton Factory. The mill leat is still visible between the weir and the viaduct over the river. The path continues along the valley before a short steep climb out of the valley to reach Hillock Farm.

From here there is a small grot spot (at the time of writing) of a derelict factory site before reaching the bank of the Leeds & Liverpool Canal. The towpath takes you back to Riley Green Bridge and a short way from the delights of the Royal Oak pub/restaurant.

Walk Directions

1. From the car park, turn right then right again to follow the minor road up to Green Lane Farm. Pass through a gate onto a field path, continue up hill ,cross a second field to reach a wood. Pass through the wood onto a track, continue straight ahead to reach a crossroads with a lodge house on the corner.

2. Continue straight on from the lodge house, follow the track around and alongside the boundary wall. Descend to a railway crossing, take care and follow the warning signs.

The lodge for Houghton Tower

3. Immediately after the crossing turn right to follow the path alongside the railway. Follow the path down to a small hamlet at Houghton Bottoms.

4. The path joins a road, bear right to follow the road, turn right at the waymarker off the road to join a path back under the railway viaduct. Follow the riverside path under the railway viaduct and past a weir. Shortly after the weir , cross a small

The weir on the River Darwen

footbridge .Continue on the path over the water meadows .

5. Climb the path right up through a wood, pass through a gate onto a field path, cross this diagonally left, then through another gate, head towards Hilltop Farm and cross a stile to reach a farm track

6. The track leads onto the main A674 road, turn left, pass the row of terraced houses, cross over and turn right onto a path. Follow the signs through a derelict factory site. the path zig zags through woodland to reach the tow path of the Leeds- Liverpool Canal.

7. Turn right to follow the canal, passing under two bridges and a small marina just before the A 675 road bridge.

8. Climb the path up to the road and turn right to follow the road which brings you back to Riley Green and the Royal Oak pub.

The Leeds & Liverpool Canal at Riley Green

WALK 6

Osbaldeston and the River Ribble

A great local walk in the Ribble Valley with a variety of landscapes and the grand Osbaldeston Hall on the banks of the River Ribble

ROUTE SUMMARY	Park Gate – Balderstone – Jackson's Banks – River Ribble - Osbaldeston Hall
START	Park Hall crossroads at a layby on Osbaldeston Lane
LOCATION & ATTRIBUTES	
Distance and Grading	5½ Miles 341 Feet (104 Mt's) ascent Easy
Route conditions	Mainly level, with field paths, a few stiles, one steep stretch of many steps, some quiet lane walking
Postcode	BB2 7LT
Grid Reference	SD 646331
Refreshments	Bay Horse on the A59 near Osbaldeston (not on route)
Car parking	Layby on Osbaldeston Lane
Toilets	None on the route

Directions to the walk

Leave the M6 at junction 31, follow the A59 towards Clitheroe. After 3 miles turn left at the Bay Horse pub onto Osbaldeston Lane, follow to a sharp left bend at a junction, turn right for Osbaldeston Green. Follow the road for ½ Mile. The lay by is just before a cross roads on the left.

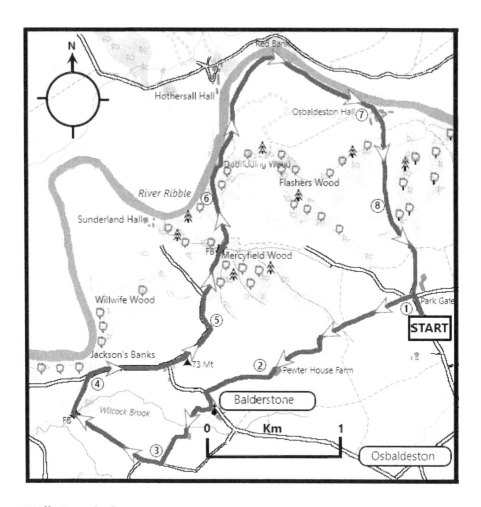

Walk Description

   The walk starts from the tiny hamlet at Osbaldeston Green and follows a little used path across flat pasture land to reach another hamlet at Balderstone with its elegant church spire of St. Leonards. From here tracks and paths lead on across farmland before a sharp short descent to cross Wilcock Brook at Daisy Hill. The route then takes you back up to Jacksons Banks Road before reaching the farmhouses at Lane Ends. A trig pillar sits beside the road in a field, the map shows an elevation of just 73Mts.

   Shortly after a path leads away to descend a mini gorge in Mercyfield Wood. Care must be taken on the steeply stepped path leading down to the footbridge and back up slippery steps.

Coming out of the wood the path leads across more open fields before entering Dobridding Wood where the path descends to emerge from the wood to reveal the majestic River Ribble. The bank of the river is followed upstream around one of the loops of the river to arrive at the grand old hall of Osbaldeston... a 16c grade 2 listed building. From here a quiet rural country lane is followed back to your car.

Walk Directions

1. Walk to the crossroads, turn left to follow unclassified road, then turn left off road onto the waymarked path cross a ditch then at a corner bear left and right to follow the boundary hedge

2. At Pewter House Farm continue through the farm onto the entrance track (Carr Lane) to reach Common Lane. Turn left follow for 100 Mt's then turn right at St Leonard's Church. Follow road past a primary school, continue onto unmade track. Cross Wilcock Brook and follow track past Hubbersty Fold farm. At a junction of tracks, turn sharp right onto track between hedges. In a few Mts., at a gate, turn left and cross the field diagonally reach the opposite corner.

3. Cross a stile and turn right, follow the track. At a sharp left bend, cross a stile to continue straight on alongside a ditch. Continue to follow the path across several field boundaries.

4. Cross the bridge over Wilcock Brook and bear right uphill ,follow the field path above the tree line to reach a stile onto Jacksons Bank Road.

Footbridge over Wilcock Brook

35

5. Turn right, follow the road to Balderstone Road junction, continue straight onto Nightfield Lane, A trig point pillar may be seen on the right of the lane.

6. Pass through the waymarked gate on the right at a left hand bend and follow the field path downhill.
Descend the steep steps and cross the brook then climb the steps through Merryfield Wood to emerge onto a field path. Cross the field and pass through Dobridding Wood to reach the bank of the River Ribble.

7. Continue to follow the bankside path. Cross a small bridge opposite the farm at Hothersall Hall, continue along the curving bank to Osbaldeston Hall.

The River Ribble at Hothersall

8. Turn right to pass through the farmyard at the hall. Continue onto the entrance drive uphill .At the end of the drive pass a riding centre to reach the crossroads and car park layby.

Osbaldeston Hall

WALK 7

Ribchester and the Ribble Valley

Starting from the Roman Fort village of Ribchester, following paths through Lancashire's rural landscape with great views over the River Ribble

ROUTE SUMMARY	Ribchester – Frances Green - Alston Reservoirs – Meadow Head – Hothersall Hall
START	Public car park at Ribchester

LOCATION & ATTRIBUTES	
Distance and Grading	7 Miles 392Feet (120Mt's) ascent moderate
Route conditions	A few stiles and field paths with a couple of steep but short inclines.
Postcode	PR3 3YE
Grid Reference	SD 648352
Refreshments	Potters barn café near car park
Car parking	Public car park off Church street in Ribchester Barrowford
Toilets	Toilets at car park

Directions to the walk

Leave the M6 at junction 31, follow the A59 towards Clitheroe. After a roundabout at Mellor Brook , turn left at the next set of traffic lights onto the B6245 for Ribchester. Follow the road into Ribchester, turn left at a T junction ,follow brown signs for Roman Museum and car park.

37

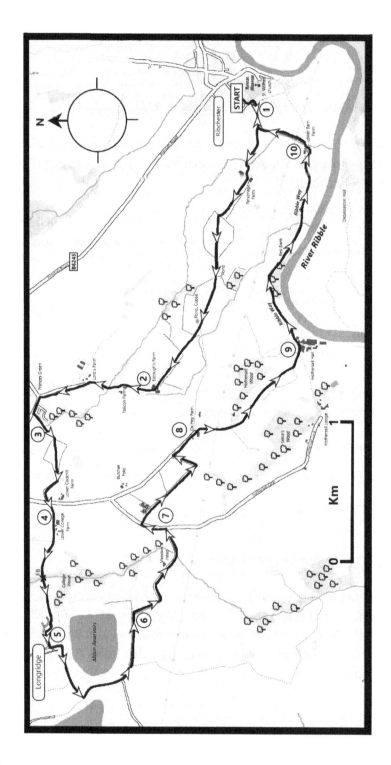

Walk Description

A straightforward walk which follows mostly well defined paths and tracks, a great one for the grandstand views of the River Ribble . The walk follows a farm tracks and paths through rural countryside towards Alston at Longridge then past the reservoirs before the return through beautiful scenery and views over the Ribble Valley ,passing the old Hothershall Hall.
The last leg is along The Ribble Way which has great views from Red Bank over the winding River Ribble before bringing you back to Ribchester. The paths may be muddy after a rainy spell, but there are few stiles (a couple of footbridges have a low bar at their ends). The route is fairly level , but one steep stretch down to the river needs care.

Walk directions

1. From the car park, turn right ,follow the road past the tennis courts area, turn right onto a broad track , follow on to Parsonage Farm. After crossing a brook, and a sharp left bend ,turn right onto a path and follow across 3 fields, at a small pond/copse bear right at a fork to pass across a boundary and cross a field path to reach a farm track. Follow to Eatough's Farm.

2. Carry on to the farm then turn right to follow the track from the farm and past Falicon Farm. Carry on past the farm on the tarmac road passing Lords Farm to reach Preston Road at Frances Green and turn left, follow a few metres then turn left onto a track just past a bus stop.

3. Follow the waymarked track bending right at a gate, cross the field diagonally to the boundary trees and follow to the right to reach another track which leads onto another gate and Hothershall Lane.

4. Cross the lane to pass through a gate opposite onto a tarmac drive follow and bear right on a track to pass the buildings of Lower College Farm. Cross a track to follow a path bearing right across a field and through a wood with a footbridge over a brook. Continue on across another field path to reach Alston Grange. Bear left around the buildings onto a track. Turn right through the farm and follow left to the entrance drive.

Footbridge at Alston Grange

5. Turn left to reach reservoir perimeter track, and turn right. Follow the track to a T junction and turn left, continue to follow the perimeter track around the reservoir , bear left at a junction onto a private road , turn off left onto a path alongside a hedge to reach a junction of tracks.

6. Bear right through a gate past a small pond and continue alongside a hedge on your right. Pass through a gate and turn left to follow the field boundary to a gate pass through onto a public footpath passing private housing at Meadow Head on the right between the fences. Continue to the road, and turn left. Follow a 100Mts. and turn right onto a waymarked drive.

7. Continue on the drive past Welsh House Cottage to follow straight onto a path between field boundaries to reach a small pond. Turn left across a footbridge and follow the path to a T junction and turn right onto a track. Follow the track to Ox Hey Farm.

Hothersall Hall

8. Follow the track past the farm ,at a fork bear right. Carry straight on at a crossways, follow the track through a gate and continue on down hill to reach Hothersall Hall. The views open up over the River Ribble as you descend the field path.

9. At the junction of paths turn left onto the Ribble Way passing the grand looking Hothersall Hall. Leave the track to continue straight on uphill above the treeline to Red Bank, then follow the boundary around the woodland to descend sharply towards the river bank. Continue along the Ribble Way on the track to Lower Barn Farm.

10. From the farm bear left onto path across a small footbridge then follow a ditch up to another track and turn right to follow the track back to the car park.

WALK 8

Hurst Green River Ramble

A pastoral walk following the Ribble and Hodder riverside then onto the pristine park like grounds of the historical Stoneyhurst College

ROUTE SUMMARY	Hurst Green – Ribble Way – Winkley Hall - Old Cromwell Bridge – Stoneyhurst College
START	The Avenue at Hurst Green
LOCATION & ATTRIBUTES	
Distance and Grading	6 ¾ Miles 520 Ft (128 Mt's) ascent Moderate
Route conditions	The paths are generally easy and level with some short steep stepped stretches. A few stiles and some muddy stretches.
Postcode	BB7 9QE
Grid Reference	SD 685380
Refreshments	The Shireburn Arms on Whalley Road, Hurst Green
Toilets	Public toilets on Avenue Road

Directions to the walk

Leave the M6 at junction 31A, follow the B6243 for 10 Miles through Longridge and on to Hurst Green. Turn left at the Shireburn Arms onto The Avenue for roadside parking.

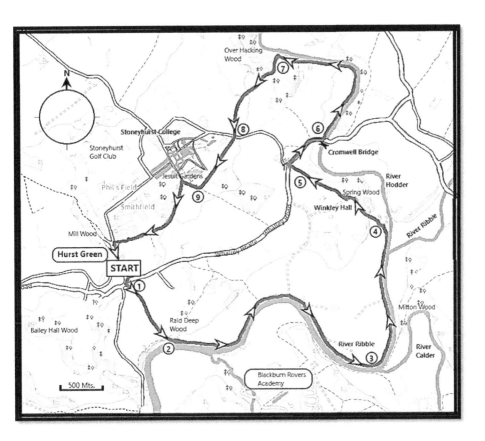

Walk Description

Starting from the idyllic village of Hurst Green, the path down to the River Ribble quickly takes you into the superb scenery of the Ribble Valley. The river runs 75 miles from North Yorkshire rising near the famous Ribblehead Viaduct and flows out to the Irish Sea between Lytham St. Anne's and Southport.

The route joins the Ribble Way and follows a great curve of the river passing tributaries joining the river on the opposite bank. First is the small Park Brook, then shortly after, the River Calder which rises from the Cliviger Gorge and flows through Burnley, Padiham and Whalley. The path turns north and shortly the Ribble is joined by the River Hodder, which flows for 23 miles from White Hill in the Bowland Fells. The path continues upstream to reach Winkley Farm where the riverside path

43

deviates up through woodland and a view point over the Lower Hodder Bridge and the ancient Cromwell Bridge.

A quiet road down may be followed to the ancient, now unused bridge, which may with care, be inspected before moving on. This is a packhorse bridge which got its name after Oliver Cromwell who marched across the bridge with his parliamentary army on their way from Gisburn to fight the King's men in the Battle of Preston in 1648.

The riverside path is rejoined and followed until a sharp left takes you steeply up a long set of steps then across open farmland to reach the estate around Stoneyhurst College.

Stonyhurst Hall was founded by Richard Shireburn in 1592 and the family lived there for 200 years. In 1794 The Hall and estate was given to the Society of Jesus as a new home for their college. The College is now a leading Catholic boarding school.and is now famous for JRR Tolkien who spent a lot of his time walking in the Ribble Valley while visiting his son at Stonyhurst College. It was during his visits that Tolkien got his inspiration for his imaginary landscape for his books Lord of the Rings and The Hobbit. The walk follows a track past the beautiful grounds of the college to return to Hurst Green.

Walk Directions

1. Cross Whalley Road at the Shireborne Arms and follow the short road past the pub car park onto a footpath. Follow the field boundary on to steep steps down to the river.

2. Turn left to follow the path, the Ribble Way, shortly passing a pipe bridge spanning the river. The path is joined by a track, continue along the track following the river.

3. At a gate, leave the track and continue to follow the riverside path which bends sharply left to the North.

4. At Winkley Hall Farm bear left, then bear right between buildings across a bridge, follow the track up through the wood. These are thegrounds of Winkley Hall. Turn right through the gate to cross 2

44

fields. Continue along the field boundary to a kissing gate onto Whalley Road.

The packhorse bridge on the River Hodder

5. Turn right to follow Whalley Road down to Lower Hodder Bridge.

6. At Lower Hodder Bridge you may wish to inspect the ancient packhorse bridge known as Cromwell's Bridge before continuing left along the riverside path on the Hodder. Follow the path as the river bends left and soon a weir is passed and Hodder Hall comes into view. Ignore a path junction near the hall and continue on the now woodland path, climbing above the river.

7. Descend to cross a small stone bridge and turn left to follow the path up then steeply down to a footbridge. Climb the steep steps and, follow the field boundary to reach a track. Continue along the track to a junction at Knowles Brow

8. At the road junction turn left then right onto track marked Stoneyhurst. Carry on straight ahead at a crossroads.

9. At a second crossroads turn right, follow the road to the observatory and

The stone bridge at point7

turn left through a gate and onto a path alongside a field boundary. Bear right keep following the hedge on your right crossing a couple of fields to reach terraced cottages at Smithy Brow. Turn right at the end of the road onto Avenue Road and the car park.

Stoneyhurst College

WALK 9

Barrowford and Blacko Hill Loop

A gentle walk with a watery theme of rivers, reservoirs and a stretch of the Leeds and Liverpool Canal around Blacko Hill.

ROUTE SUMMARY	Barrowford – Waters Meeting – Blacko Water – Admergill - Admergill Pasture – Foulridge Tunnel – Leeds Liverpool Canal
START	Car park on Colne Road, Barrowford

LOCATION & ATTRIBUTES	
Distance and Grading	6 Miles 719Feet (219Mt's) ascent moderate
Route conditions	Quite a few stiles, and field paths a couple of steep but short inclines. The path can be rough and get muddy in places
Postcode	BB9 6JQ
Grid Reference	SD 863398
Refreshments	Pendle Heritage Centre cafe opposite the car park
Car parking	Public car park on Colne Road, Barrowford
Toilets	At the Heritage Centre

Directions to the walk

Leave the M65 at junction 14, follow the A6068 towards Keighley. Turn left at the next set of traffic lights onto the B6247. Follow the road to Barrowford, look out for the car park entrance 400 Mts. past the canal bridge on your right.

47

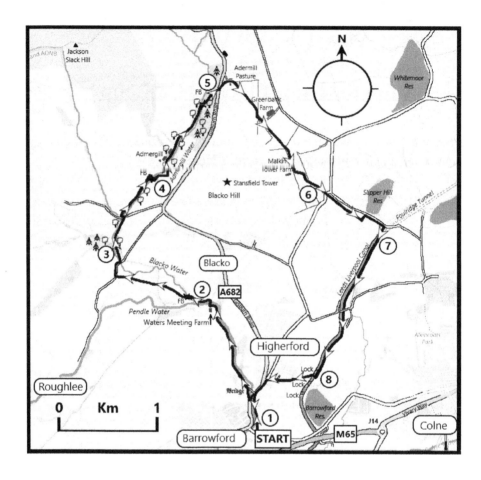

Walk Description

This walk has the advantage of starting a couple of miles from a motorway junction. The route gets off in good style by leaving the pretty village of Barrowford past an ancient packhorse bridge, following The Pendle Way alongside Pendle Water. Soon the path reaches Waters Meeting where Blacko Water joins Pendle Water.(This is the furthest point of Walk 10). The course of Blacko Water is followed up to Blacko Foot before turning to follow the Admergill Water up stream to skirt around the prominent Blacko Hill with its remarkable folly tower built in 1890 by a local grocer Johnathan Stansfield to give him a better view over Ribblesdale.

48

The grand views over the tranquil landscape open up with meadowlands, gently sloping hills and farmsteads. A stiff climb brings you out onto Admergill Pasture where the route gently descends towards Slipper Hill Reservoir. From here the route descends to the western portal of the famous Foulridge Tunnel on the Leeds and Liverpool Canal. The towpath is followed to reach the locks at Barrowford, then a short walk returns you to the car park

There is a true story of a cow that fell into the canal at the Barrowford end of the tunnel and swam through the tunnel to the Foulridge end. The exhausted swimmer was revived with alcohol and a photograph can be seen in the nearby Hole in the Wall pub. A great walk with variety of scenery and historical interest, not too arduous and very pleasant scenery

Walk directions

1. Leave the car park at back left corner, take the riverside path right, alongside Pendle Water, turn left onto the main road to cross the river then turn right onto Foreside to pass the ancient Higherford Old Bridge. Carry on to the riverside path (Pendle Way). Continue on through a gate past the Old Oak Tree Cottage. Continue on to reach Waters Meeting Farm at a farmtrack bridge.

Footbridge over Blacko Water

2. Turn right to cross the bridge then left onto the riverside path, bear right at the confluence of the Blacko and Pendle Waters. Cross the footbridge over Blacko Water and climb the gently ascending field path across two fields and stiles, continue on alongside a field boundary to reach Blacko Foot Farm.

3. Pass the farm and turn right onto the road, at a road bridge, turn left through a gate, to follow the riverside path, pass a footbridge on the left and continue on to reach a road bridge.
   Climb steps then cross the road, turn left over bridge then descend to cross a footbridge and continue on the riverside path alongside the Admergill Water. Cross a footbridge over the river and turn left on a road which leads to Admergill Farm.

4. At a gate onto the road there is a view of the Stansfield Tower on Blacko Hill. Turn left down to the farm. Continue on past the farm to reach a gate and stile. Cross and continue to follow the riverside path to another footbridge, cross and climb the bank to reach the A682 road.

The A682 crossing with the Stansfield Tower in view

5. Pass through a gate and cross carefully, turn left and follow a few Mt's then pass through a wall stile and ascend the opposite bank. Pass along a wall and enter the farmstead of Admergill Pasture. Pass between the cottages then bear right and look out for a small gate in the wall on the right.

Cross the meadow diagonally left uphill, then two further fields to reach a wall and follow to the right. Cross a wall stile on the left and follow the fence to another stile at a gate near Greenbank Farm, cross and continue straight on alongside a wall and straight on down where the wall ends. Drop down a small clough to reach a gate, pass and continue alongside a wall. Bear left near a farm (marked Malkin Tower), diagonally left from the wall to reach the opposite wall, and bear right to follow to a broken wall stile. Cross and bear left across the field to reach a stile behind a cottage.

6. Pass through the cottage garden, cross the road and pass through the wall stile opposite and follow the waymarked wooded path downhill to reach a private house. Turn left to skirt the gardens and cross the access bridge onto Slipper Road. Turn right to follow the road downhill to cross the bridge over Wanless Water then turn right onto the waymarked track which leads you to the south portal of Foulridge Tunnel.

7. Continue onto the towpath from the canal tunnel, follow on to the Borrowford Locks.

8. Cross the footbridge over the locks and across the field path to Francis Avenue. Turn left at the end of the road, then left again onto the A682. Follow 150

Footbridge at Barrowford Locks

Mt's towards the bridge and turn left onto the footpath just before the bridge to reach the car park.

WALK 10
Barley, Blacko and Waters Meeting

A delightful mixture of hillside and waterside paths, commanding grand views of the sylvan countryside between Pendle Hill and Blacko Hill.

ROUTE SUMMARY	Barley – Roughlee – Waters Meeting - Blacko Foot – Hollin Top – White Hough
START	Barley, The Avenue Car Park

LOCATION & ATTRIBUTES	
Distance and Grading	5 ½ Miles - 781 Ft (231 Mt's) ascent easy
Route conditions	The route follows mostly well used paths and tracks with a few gentle inclines and a few stiles.
Postcode	BB12 9JU
Grid Reference	SD 823404
Refreshments	The Cabin at the car park; Pendle Inn in Barley
Car parking	Public car park
Toilets	At the car park

Directions to the walk

Leave the M65 at Junction 8, follow the A6068 towards Padiham, shortly after passing Higham, turn left onto St. Anne's Way. Follow the signs for Newchurch, carry on through Newchurch, and follow brown signs for Barley picnic site. The Avenue car park is on the right after crossing Barley Bridge

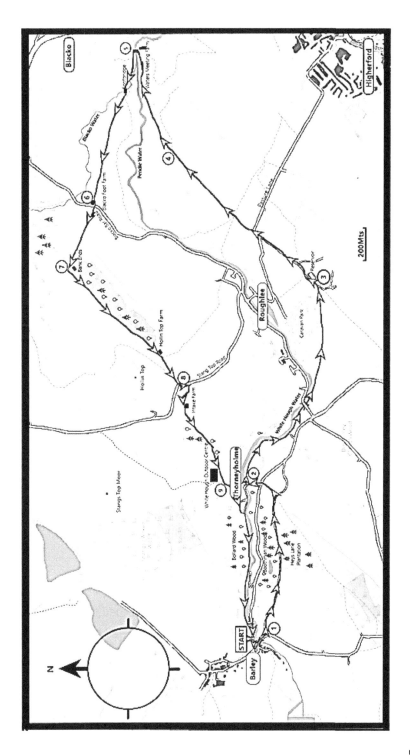

53

Walk Description

The walk starts off by crossing White Hough Water, which for some reason becomes Pendle Water at Roughlee. The route follows a track climbing gently above the river and shortly a rear view of the Big End of Pendle Hill will be seen looming over the village of Barley.

Further along the track, the first of many views of the Stansfield Tower on Blacko Hill appears. This was built in 1890 as a folly, to provide a local grocer with a grandstand view over Ribblesdale, sadly this was not quite achieved.

The route then drops down to a bridge over the White Hough Water where a delightful riverside path is followed through Thornyholme and onto Roughlee these are small hamlets of scattered cottages strung along the valley of the river which is now called Pendle Water.

There follows a climb up to a low ridge with commanding views over Pendle Forest and the ridge path is followed before dropping down to the Waters Meeting Farm .So called after the nearby confluence of the Blacko and Pendle Waters. This is the turning point of the walk, crossing the river, the route turns back to follow Blacko Water for a short distance before gently ascending to Blacko Foot Farm and on to Bank Ends. The route turns south west to climb the ridge path up to Brown Hill which is skirted via Hollin Top Farm. There is always a view to be appreciated on the walk, Pendle Hill dominates on this stretch.

The path drops down from here to another track past Intake Farm then on through woodland to reach the large White Hough Outdoor Centre. This is a live in centre for all outdoor activities such as canoeing, abseiling and climbing.

The walk is completed by following the Narrowgates track past the pretty mill cottages, home to the Narrowgates Mill workers which closed in 1967.

Walk Directions

1. Leave the car park, turn right onto the main road then left across Barley Bridge over White Hough Waters then left again to follow Hays Lane. After 500 Mts. turn left off the track at a sharp right bend onto a steep downhill path to reach Barley New Road, cross over and follow the track down to the bridge over White Hough Water.

54

Big end of Pendle Hill seen from Hey's Lane

2. Turn right to follow the delightful riverside path to Blacko Bar Road, cross over and continue along the path. Follow the path as it moves away from the river and climb gently up on a field path passing above a caravan site and woodland to reach a reservoir and track at Ridgaling Farm.

3. Turn left, following the tarmac road to a junction, bear left to follow the lane to Pasture Lane at a junction with a sharp bend. Cross the road to pass through a gate opposite and continue onto a field path following the wall on the ridge with great views over Pendle Water

Footpath off Pasture Lane

55

Hollin Top can be seen, which lies on the return leg of the route.

4. Cross the field boundary wall at a gate and continue alongside the wall Follow the path into a small wood and continue on to emerge on a descending path to the Waters Meeting Farm.

Waters Meeting: The confluence of Blacko and Pendle Waters

5. Turn left over the Pendle Water Farm track access bridge then left again onto another path, following the river to the confluence of Blacko Water and Pendle Water. Take a while to savour this lovely tranquil spot before moving off alongside the Blacko Water to reach a footbridge over the river.

Cross the bridge and climb the gently ascending field path across two fields and stiles, continue on alongside a field boundary to reach Blacko Foot Farm.

6. Follow the track to a tarmacked road, cross and continue straight ahead onto another farm track. This track leads onto Bank Ends Farm. The right of way lies on the right of the track and parallels it up to a wood.

7. At Bank Ends the path bends left to another track, turn right then shortly left onto a field path leading out of the wood uphill. Pass through a gate then onto another field path passing woodland on your left, then alongside a wall which leads to an isolated barn. Skirt left and follow the path on to reach the farmstead of Hollin Top. Pass through the farmyard onto the access track and follow this down to Stang Top Road.

8. Turn left to follow the road downhill a few strides then turn right onto the access track to Intake Farm. The right of way follows a path around the back of the farmhouse on your right. The path then leads steeply down to enter a woodland, and onto a track which continues out of the wood and down to a junction.

9. Turn left and follow the track through the White Hough Outdoor Centre.   Keep left in the complex and then turn right onto Narrowgates Cottages. Follow this track back to Barley, passing the old mill cottages near the end.

WALK 11

Bolton by Bowland to Sawley

A walk following paths along watercourses between the villages with great views of typical Ribble Valley scenery

ROUTE SUMMARY	Bolton by Bowland – Holden - Bolton Peel – Rodhill Gate – Sawley – Bolton Hall
START	Car park at Bolton by Bowland
LOCATION & ATTRIBUTES	
Distance and Grading	6 Miles 546Feet (166Mt's) ascent moderate
Route conditions	Mainly level with a few stiles . some roadside walking and a couple of short steep stretches
Postcode	BB7 4NQ
Grid Reference	SD 784493
Refreshments	Tea room next to the car park, and The Spread Eagle Inn at Sawley
Car parking	Public car park next to Skirden Bridge at Bolton by Bowland
Toilets	As above

Directions to the walk

Leave the M6 at junction 51, follow the A59 towards Skipton. Turn left after 12 miles for Sawley. Follow the road over the River Ribble and turn right for Settle. At a junction in Holden at Copy Nook Hotel, turn right , follow the road to Bolton by Bowland , the car park is immediately after crossing the bridge ito Bolton by Bowland on the right.

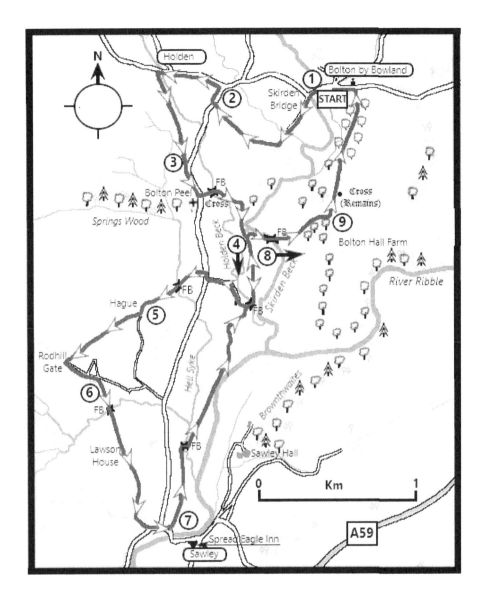

Walk Description

  The pretty stone built village of Bolton-by-Bowland lies on the eastern
edge of Forest of Bowland. This walk starts here and makes an irregular
  figure of eight circular course along the valley formed by the River Ribble
and its tributaries of Holden Beck.and Skirden Beck The route's furthest
point is at the equally attractive village of Sawley where a small detour can

be made to view the remains of a Cistercian abbey originating from the 12th century. Parts of the route follows Holden Beck, the River Ribble and Skirden Beck, by criss-crossing the valley between the two villages. The walk is mainly through open pleasant level countryside, its easy going but be prepared for some muddy conditions. The valley is a verdant green landscape dotted with trees and surrounded by the round topped Bowland Fells, to the south lies the familiar profile of Pendle Hill.

Towards the end of the walk the route follows the drive through the parkland of Bolton Hall with lovely views down over the Skirden Beck and where the remains of an ancient cross, although only the stone plinth can be seen. Finally, at Bolton by Bowland there is a distinguished church of St. Peter and St Paul with its grand looking tower. There are also a war memorial and the old village cross and stocks, before a welcome refreshment break at the tea room next the car park

Walk directions

1. Leave the car park turn left cross the Skirden Bridge and turn left onto the waymarked road, follow the road, cross a stream and at a sharp left bend, turn right through a kissing gate onto a field path. Follow the path uphill along the left hand boundary to reach a farmstead at Barrett Hill Brow.

2. Turn right follow the road to Copy Nook Hotel and turn left onto Holden Road. Follow the road into Holden, bear left at a fork for Lane Ends, cross the Holden Beck, then turn left through a waymarked gate onto a track. Bear left at a fork and follow the tree lined Beck. Cross a field boundary and continue diagonally across

The ancient cross on Bolton by Bowland Road

the middle of a second field path to reach steps down to a road.

3. Turn right, follow the road to Bolton Peel Farm and the ancient cross on the roadside. The old stone farm houses are rather grand looking with mullioned windows. Turn back a few Mts. and turn right through a waymarked gate in the wall, drop down to a field path. Follow the field boundary on your left to reach a footbridge over the Holden Beck Cross and turn right, skirting the field to reach a gate and track, turn right, follow the track between woodlands to a crossway.

4. Continue on through a kissing gate and follow the field boundary with Holden Beck and a line of trees on your right, cross a stile, then continue on to a footbridge, cross and bear right up to a track at an isolated house, turn right to follow the access track to return to the Bolton by Bowland road. Turn right for a few Mt's then turn left, cross a stile and follow a field path, bearing left, head for the farmstead of Hague. Cross a footbridge over Hell Syke and continue to the farm complex.

5. Pass through a gate to the farmyard, bear right then left to pass between the buildings, note the large wishing well? (or elaborate fodder shelter) as you leave the farmyard, and turn right through a gate, cross a field path through a second gate and cross another field to the opposite corner, cross a stile and continue onto another ascending field path to reach a farmhouse at Rodhill Gate. Turn left, follow the tarmac track downhill to a sharp left bend.

6. Continue straight on down, ignore the hairpin track on the left, carry straight on alongside trees, then turn right at the junction of tracks through a gate, follow the path alongside the left hand boundary. Pass through a gate on the left and continue alongside the opposite boundary. Drop down to cross a footbridge and continue up to reach the farmstead at Lawson House. Pass through the farmyard between buildings and through a gate onto a rough track. Follow on down to a woodland and follow the path alongside the wood to reach a junction, turn left past attractive stone housing called Green End. Follow the tarmac road to Sawley Bridge. Turn left on the main road. At a junction turn right towards the bridge.

At this point you may decide to take a break at the Spread Eagle Inn which is 200 Mts. across the bridge

7. Turn left just before the bridge to pass through a gate, follow a field path alongside the left boundary hedge. Cross a footbridge over Hell Syke and continue to follow the path, bearing right towards the river. (Follow the coned path do not be tempted to follow the river bank, river bailiffs regularly patrol here). Cross a stile and continue through a new plantation, cross a track and head for a footbridge over Holden Brook (this is the same bridge on the outward leg). Climb the slight bank to cross a stile at the top. Continue to follow the Holden Beck and a narrow wood on your left to reach a crossways, turn right onto the track.

8. Follow the track, passing through a gate, as it curves right, dropping down through woodland to a ford and long footbridge over the Skirden Beck. Cross and continue to follow the track up the flank of a wooded hill.

The footbridge over Skirden Beck

9. At a junction of tracks, turn left at a gate onto the tarmacked King Edward Mews. Follow this delightful drive to return to the Bolton by

Bowland. Look out for the remains of the ancient cross on the right of the drive a few Mts. from the gate. At the entrance to the drive turn left onto the main road passing the St Peter and St Paul church and the memorial cross with stocks on the village green to return to the car park..

Entrance to King Edward Mews

WALK 12
Stocks Reservoir Circuit

A grand walk around the Stocks Reservoir set in an area of outstanding natural beauty

ROUTE SUMMARY	Gisburn Forest – River Hodder – Eak Hill – Stocks Reservoir Café – Reservoir Dam – Hole House Lane
START	School Lane car park, Gisburn Forest
LOCATION & ATTRIBUTES	
Distance and Grading	6 ½ Miles 702Feet (214 Mt's) ascent easy
Route conditions	Mostly easy well marked paths, a little roadside walking. No steep slopes or stiles
Postcode	BB7 4TS
Grid Reference	SD 732565
Refreshments	The Stocks Reservoir café (half way round)
Car parking	Car park on School Lane in Gisburn Forest
Toilets	As above

Directions to the walk

Leave the M6 at junction 51, follow the A59 towards Skipton. Turn left after 12 miles for Sawley. Follow the road over the River Ribble and turn right for Settle. At a junction in Holden at Copy Nook Hotel, turn left. Follow road signs for Slaidburn, bear right at a fork for Clapham. At a crossroads carry straight on, follow the brown signs for Gisburn.

Forest. Bear right at St James's church, cross a causeway and continue straight on, the car park is on the left at a sharp right bend.

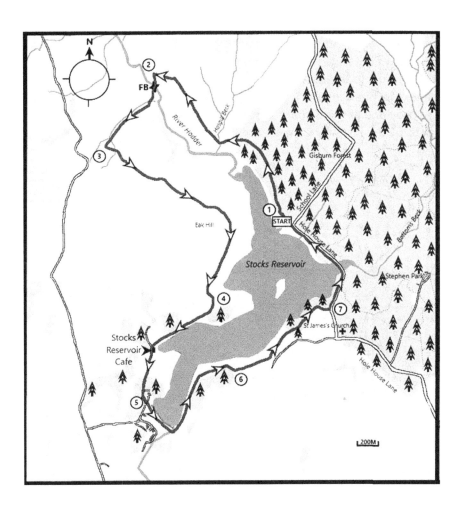

Walk Description

This moorland walk has views all around the Stocks Reservoir on well made paths that are easy to follow with few inclines and no stiles. The reservoir is located in the Forest of Bowland and a circular reservoir footpath gives walkers the to recharge their batteries in a moorland landscape with the added attraction of the large open waters of the reservoir with its abundant wildfowl and the surrounding patchwork of farmland and forestry. The reservoir is a haven for wildlife and is one of the best sites in the North West for a chance to see a wide range of wildfowl and moorland birds. Species that may be seen include Curlews, Wheatear and Meadow Pipits and many others that inhabit the area.

Gisburn Forest to the east of the reservoir has become an important recreation destination with a range of activity opportunities for locals and visitors provided at the Gisburn Forest Hub at Stephen Park which is managed by the Forestry Commission.

The bridge over Hasgill Beck

Walk Directions

1. Leave the rear of the car park, follow the broad path through forest and above the reservoir, cross the Hasgill Beck then on to reach a derelict house.

2. Bear left onto a path to descend a zig zag path to cross the River Hodder on a footbridge. Ascend the path leading past a ruin and continue up alongside a line of trees in a small clough to reach a track.

3. Turn left to follow the track, bear right at a fork and follow the track as it contours around Eak Hill above the reservoir.

Footbridge over the River Hodder

4. Continue on the main track down to the bank of the reservoir, shortly you arrive at a café and fishing club with a car park. A good place for a rest and take in the views. Continue along the access track to reach the dam and United Utilities reservoir buildings.

The view from the bank of Stocks Reservoir

5. Cross the entrance drive then cross the dam and the overflow bridge. Turn left to follow the broad path along the reservoir's south side.

6. Continue to follow the path as it enters a wood and swings right up to

View of the valve tower from the dam

join a path alongside Hole House Lane,

7. Turn left and follow the path through woodland to reach the road over the causeway. Cross and continue on the path alongside the road to return to School Lane car park.

WALK 13

Slaidburn, River Hodder and Easington Brook

This is a riverside walk following paths through superb countryside between Slaidburn and Newton with fine views of the Forest of Bowland

ROUTE SUMMARY	Slaidburn – Newton – Easington – Harrop Hall Farm Langcliff Cross – High Field Farm
START	Slaidburn, Chapel Street Public Car Park
LOCATION & ATTRIBUTES	
Distance and Grading	6 ½ Miles 518 Ft (158 Mts.) Ascent Moderate
Route conditions	The walk is on mainly good paths, be prepared for some muddy conditions and quite a few stiles! Some gentle inclines and short stretches of quiet roadside walking.
Postcode	BB7 3ES
Grid Reference	SD 713523
Refreshments	Riverbank tearooms and Hark to Bounty Inn on Chapel Street
Car parking	Public car park
Toilets	At the car park

Directions to walk

Leave the M6 at junction 31, follow the A59 towards Clitheroe. Turn off at a roundabout onto the A671 to pass through Clitheroe , at roundabout, follow signs for Waddington on the B 6478. Pass the Higher Buck on your right, keep straight on follow the road over Easington Fell to Newton. Continue right on the B 6478 to Slaidburn. The car park is on the left past the village centre.

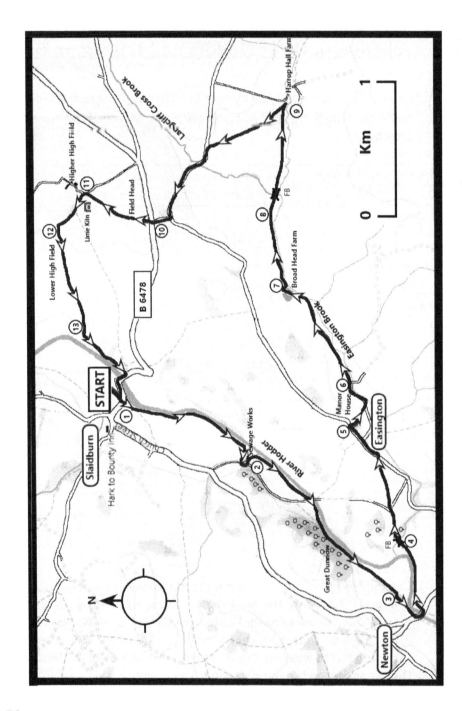

Walk Description

This walk must rate as one of the finest in the region of east Lancashire. It starts in the tranquil timeless stone village of Slaidburn where an impressive statue of a statue of a soldier, a war memorial which cannot fail to stir as you arrive in the village. From the public car park near the bridge over the River Hodder the walk follows the course of the River Hodder downstream to Newton, the views are of idyllic countryside, with a mixture of pasture land and wooded hills rising from the banks of the Hodder as it winds its way down to the River Ribble.

From Newton Bridge the walk continues by following lesser used paths along the course of the Easington Brook upstream, take your time as you may come across a Kingfisher seeking its dinner from the clear waters.

The route passes through the large farmstead at Manor House before continuing gently uphill to the open fellsides. A sharp turn north west follows at Harrop Hall farm to climb to the highest point of the walk (c. 210 Mt's) at the farmstead of High Field. A disused lime kiln is passed before descending to the River Hodder once again for the return leg to Slaidburn. Food and drink can be had at the end of this great walk at

Newton Bridge

71

the Hark to Bounty Inn. This historic building was formerly known as the Dog Inn. The name "Hark to Bounty" was derived from the master of the local hunt calling out his favourite dog's name when he heard its bark outside the Inn. The Inn has an upper room once used as the original Moot Courtroom when Slaidburn was the administrative centre of the Forest of Bowland.

Walk Directions

1. Turn right at entrance then cross road through a children's play area, at a fork keep left to follow the path alongside the River Hodder.

2. Follow the deviated path right around the small sewage works, then rejoin the riverside path. Cross a track that passes over a bridge, continue on to follow the riverside path to Great Dunnow Wood seen straight ahead. The path continues straight as the river deviate left.

The footbridge over Easington Brook

3. Cross a stile in a wall on the left and follow the wall to reach a road, turn left and follow over Newton Bridge. Cross a stile on the left and continue on the riverside path on the opposite bank of the river.

4. The path leaves the riverside, carry on to reach a ford and footbridge over Easington Brook. After passing through a small wood, follow the field boundary to a stile in the corner of a field, cross this and follow the field path diagonally across to a gate onto a minor road Turn left and follow into the hamlet of Easington

The gate and stile at Manor Farm

5. Turn right at a waymarker at the gable end of Manor House Farm, pass through the farmyard to a junction, bear left onto a winding track.

6. Turn left off the track at a bridge and cross a stile to follow a riverside path. Follow the path around a plantation away from the brook, and continue on a field path to reach Broad Heath Farm.

7. Pass through a gate then through the farmyard, turn right at a junction. In a few steps turn left through another gate to follow the brookside path.

8. Pass through another gate, continue straight on alongside a stone wall. Cross the Langcliffe Brook on a footbridge then cross a wall stile, turn right a few steps then left to continue on a the brookside path to reach a gate at Harrop Hall.

9. Do not pass through the gate. Bear sharp left uphill over the hill field path, passing over a stile between fields. Cross a stile onto a minor road and turn left to follow it to a road junction.

10. Follow the road to the B6478. Cross over and follow the farm road opposite to reach Field Head. Pass between the farm buildings, turn right at end building through a gate, follow the track cross a wall stile then continue alongside a wall to reach another track.

The disused lime kiln at Lower High Field Farm

11. Join the track and follow it to another track and bear left passing a disused lime kiln, follow the track to Lower High Field farm.

12. Keep left at a barn next to the farm to follow a brookside path. Pass through a gate and bear left at the fork to follow the faint brookside path. Pass through another two gates on field path beneath a transmission line, bear left to cross a plank bridge. Climb up a bank to pass through a gate and bear right across a field path.

13. Pass through a kissing gate and continue on path to reach the bank of the River Hodder and follow to the squeeze stile onto the road bridge, turn right to the car park at Slaidburn.

WALK 14

Beacon Fell and Bleasdale

A varied walk in Forest of Bowland countryside with great views, moorland, woodland and a delightful stretch of the River Brock.

ROUTE SUMMARY	Beacon Fell – Higher Brock Mill – Bleasdale – Brooks – High Moor – Brock Mill -
START	Beacon Fell Country Park Visitor Centre

LOCATION & ATTRIBUTES	
Distance and Grading	8 ½ Miles 958 Feet (292Mt's) ascent moderate
Route conditions	The route follows well marked paths and tracks, a little quiet roadside walking, a couple of stiles and there may be some muddy stretches, especially on the riverside path.
Postcode	PR3 2NL
Grid Reference	SD 565427
Refreshments	Café at the visitor centre
Car parking	Pay and display at the visitor centre
Toilets	At the visitor centre

Directions to the walk

Leave the M6 at junction 32, onto the M55, Use the left 2 lanes to take the A6 exit to Preston/Garstang, at the next roundabout, take the 1st exit, continue to follow the Broughton bypass until the next roundabout , take the 3rd exit onto Whittingham Ln/B5269. Go under

75

the motorway and take the 1st turning left into Langley Lane. Beacon Fell is signposted from here.

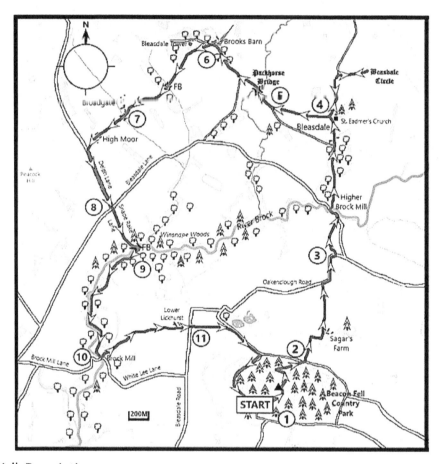

Walk Description

Although the route follows the River Brock only a fraction of the route, this walk merits inclusion in this book for it has many attractive features. The start is at the well established visitor centre with its many facilities and views at the trig point, the route visits historical heritage sites, including the Bleasdale Circle ,an ancient packhorse bridge, and a delightful stretch of the aforementioned River Brock. which once had water mills on its course.

The walk begins with a panoramic view from the trig point of the vast Lancashire plain rolling out towards the Fylde coast and Blackpool . From here a short descent through the forest on the fell gives way to quiet lanes and tracks bringing you to the tiny village of Bleasdale with its quaint square towered church sitting in an isolated spot beneath the fells of the Forest of Bowland.

From here a short detour can be made to visit the Bronze Age Circle which consists of a circle of 11 concrete posts in place of the long gone timber posts It is also referred to as a 'henge monument', the centre used to have a mound with a burial inside.

The route then follows on past an ancient pack horse bridge before reaching Brooks Barn and Bleasdale Tower.... a 19th century manor house. The field paths and tracks pass through more of the Bowland countryside with great floral displays of daffodils in spring around the farmsteads.

There is a change of scenery when the River Brock is reached at a footbridge where a path is followed through woodland alongside its meandering course, passing Paradise Cottage along the way to Brock Mill. The woodland is home to many species of bird such as greater spotted woodpeckers, nuthatches, treecreepers, long-tailed tits. dippers and grey wagtail are to be found along the course of the river.

In summer blackcap, willow warbler, chiffchaff, and garden warbler, may be seen. From Brock Mill the route continues on paths passing farmsteads and across fields ,before the gentle climb up a up a lane to return to Beacon fell .

Walk directions

1. From the car park follow the track east, then shortly turn left steeply uphill. Turn north east steeply to reach the trig point. Descend on faint path northwest downhill towards the wooded area. Turn right onto broad track passing through the trees and cross another broad path and enter the dense wood to descend down the track to reach Beacon Fell Road.

2. Cross the road and take the waymarked path opposite towards the farms in the distance, follow the left hand boundary then turn right and left past the farm. Follow the farm track to Oakenclough Road ,turn right and after rounding a right hand bend

The trig pillar on Beacon Hill

turn left to cross a stile onto a path. There are clear views of Parlick from here.

3. Follow the path alongside the left hand boundary, left then right to reach a stile and steps down to Bleasdale Lane. Turn left , follow the road to Higher Brock Mill Bridge, cross the bridge then turn right onto a Waymarked road for Bleasdale Cottages.

The packhorse bridge at Brook Bridge

4. At St Eadmer's church , continue onward up the road to Vicarage Farm and turn right through a gate onto a path to view the circle .Return to point 4 ,turn right through a gate past a barn conversion, follow the track across the moorland to a junction with a tarmac road at a copse

5. Follow the road right to Brooks Bridge, from here you may view the ancient packhorse bridge. Continue to follow the road up to Brooks Barn

6. Turn left through a gate and follow the track alongside the left hand wall, passing the impressive Bleasdale Tower. Cross a stile and bear left on a field path, cross a footbridge and through a narrow wood to join a track, and follow to Broadgate Farm

The garden at Broadgate Farm

7. Turn left at the buildings and cross the access track over a bridge and onto a track opposite to pass the farmhouse gardens on your right. Follow the left field boundary to a gate, cross and continue to follow the path to skirt around on the right of the High Moor farm. Turn right on the farm access track then turn left on Delph Lane.

8. At a crossroads ,carry straight on crossing Bleasdale Lane onto Snape Rake Lane. At the end of the lane , cross a footbridge and turn right onto a brookside track

9. Pass the well named Paradise Cottage continue on a track then follow the riverside path. Join the drive at Brock Mill, follow around the grand looking houses .

10. Bear left before the entrance and cattle grid, continue uphill then bear right off the drive onto a track alongside woodland, bear right at the end of the wood , continue to follow the right hand boundary, cross a track and head for the farm at Lower Lickhurst .Skirt

Paradise Cottage

around right of the farm to reach the drive to Bleasdale Road.

11. Cross Bleasdale Road at the entrance and follow the waymarked track almost opposite to pass Middle Lickhurst farm, continue to follow the field path alongside the boundary ,cross another field to reach a footbridge onto North Nook Lane. Turn right ,follow the road to a junction , bear right and follow the road uphill to return to the visitor centre and car park

WALK 15

Garstang to Churchtown

This easy walk follows parts of the Rivers Wyre and Calder, and a pretty stretch of the Lancaster Canal.

ROUTE SUMMARY	Garstang – Churchtown – River Wyre – River Calder – Lancaster Canal
START	Garstang High Street car park
LOCATION & ATTRIBUTES	
Distance and Grading	7 ¾ Miles – 219 Feet (67 Mts.) ascent - Easy
Route conditions	Mostly on good level paths and tracks but some muddy conditions to be expected. A couple of short stretches of road walking
Postcode	PR3 1EB
Grid Reference	SD493454
Refreshments	The Crown on the High Street (great fish and chips) The Punchbowl in Churchtown (half way round)
Car parking	Garstang High Street car park
Toilets	See above pubs

Directions to the walk

Leave the M6 at junction 32 onto the M55 then leave this at junction 1, follow the A 6 toward Garstang, continue on the A6 for 7 miles, turn right onto the B6430 for Garstang. After about a mile, cross the River Wyre bridge and, follow the B6430 road signs for the High Street car park.

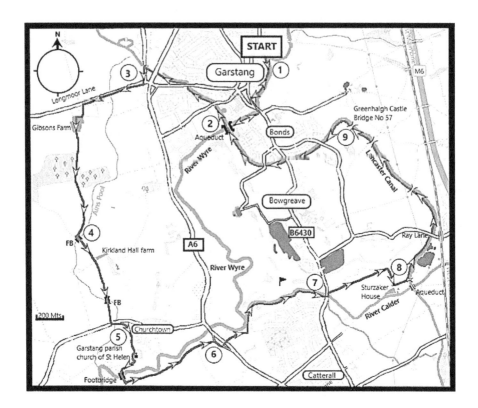

Walk Description

This is a walk with a watery theme as follows the water courses that abound around Garstang. Paths are followed alongside parts of the Rivers Wyre and Calder, as well as a pretty stretch of the Lancaster Canal.

Being a flat landscape with a risk of flooding, dykes have been built to protect the farmland. Once out of the urban area of Garstang the countryside soon reveals itself with wide views and peacefulness. Many farms are passed and there are brooks and wooded areas before the half way point of the pretty village of Churchtown and its St Helens church next to the River Wyre, an ideal spot for a break.

Restarting, the river is crossed and followed for a stretch before reaching the town of Catteral and the confluence of the Rivers Wyre and Calder. The latter is then followed on a riverside path before striding off across more farmland paths to reach the Lancaster Canal once more.

The canal towpath is rejoined as it meanders north and west to return to the aqueduct at Garstang and the riverside path back to the car park.

Although a flattish walk there are quite a few stiles and the paths can get muddy, but there are no steep inclines, except for the climb up the steps of the aqueduct! There is a stretch of roadside walking where care is needed and single file is advisable.

Walk Directions

1. From the rear of the car park and follow the riverside path to reach a short road leading onto the main road through Garstang. Turn left to cross the bridge then cross the road to reach steps down past the old corn mill. Go through the mill entrance and onto the riverside path.

2. The path leads to an aqueduct, pass under and climb to reach the Lancaster Canal then follow the canal towpath north. Pass a marina on the far bank and under several bridges including the distinctive white arched bridge for a water pipe.

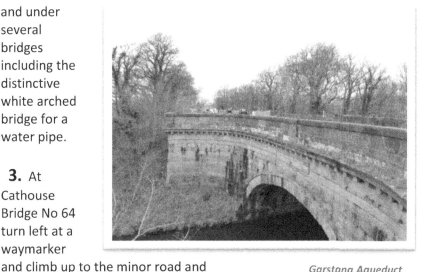

Garstang Aqueduct

3. At Cathouse Bridge No 64 turn left at a waymarker and climb up to the minor road and turn right to follow the road to a crossroads and turn right. Follow the road (Longmoor Lane) for 1/4 mile. Pass Park farm where cute calves may be seen in little shelters on the field opposite, then at Gibson's farm turn left to follow the waymarked track through the farm. Carry on along the track, pass through a gate and shortly turn right and left around a wood.

4. Carry on alongside a brook on a field path to a footbridge, turn left to cross this and continue to follow the track which leads onto another track from the left. Carry straight on to emerge at Kirkland Hall Farm and a crossroads, carry straight on, follow the track crossing a bridge to the main road.

5. Turn left and cross the road to join Ainspool Lane and follow to the pretty village centre of Churchtown, bear right at the memorial to reach St Helens Church, a good place for a break. Restart by following the path around the church to reach the

The memorial at Churchtown

River Wyre and a footbridge, cross over the river and turn left at Catterall Hall Farm to follow a track past Arnwood House and onward to reach a housing estate.

6. Turn right to follow the minor road a few yards and turn left past a car park and through a gate to reach a main road. Cross the road and continue onto Tan Yard road directly opposite. Follow the road around 150 mts. and turn left on a path between industrial units. The path soon passes the confluence of the Rivers Wyre and Calder, follow the path alongside the River Calder, with a golf course on the opposite bank.

7. The path ends at Calder Bridge, turn left over the road bridge, then immediately after turn right onto the waymarked path. Follow the boundary hedge crossing 3 fields to reach a track and turn right. Follow the track to reach the Sturzaker House complex and turn left to follow the track to the Lancaster Canal.

8. From the road bridge, drop down to the towpath on the right then turn left to pass under the bridge and follow the canal all the way back to Garstang.

9. A sharp left bend in the canal follows Greenhalgh Castle Bridge (No 57) which is passed before reaching the aqueduct No 61. Descend the steps at the aqueduct and return along the riverside path through the mill complex, cross the main road, and turn left, turn right at the mini roundabout, follow the road a few yards then turn right to follow the sign for the riverside path back to the car park

Bridge 53 on the Lancaster Canal

WALK 16

Scorton, Dolphinholme and Wyresdale

Walking a stretch of the meandering Wyre Way through a maze of lakes from Scorton to Dolphinholme ,before returning through scenic Wyresdale

ROUTE SUMMARY	Scorton – Wyre Lake – Coreless Mill – Dolphinholme – Street - Foxhouses – Wyresdale Park
START	The Barn in Scorton
LOCATION & ATTRIBUTES	
Distance and Grading	7½ Miles 516 Feet (157 Mt's) ascent Moderate
Route conditions	Mainly level, with field paths, a few stiles, a few stiles some quiet lane walking
Postcode	PR3 1AU
Grid Reference	SD 501487
Refreshments	The Barn in Scorton; Applestore café in Wyresdale
Car parking	Free parking at the Barn in Scorton
Toilets	See above refreshment stops

Directions to the walk

Leave the M6 at junction 33, take first exit at a roundabout, follow the A6 towards Preston. After 3 miles past an Esso garage turn left onto Station Lane, follow over a narrow bridge to Scorton Village. Turn right, the entrance to The Barn is a few Mt's on the right.

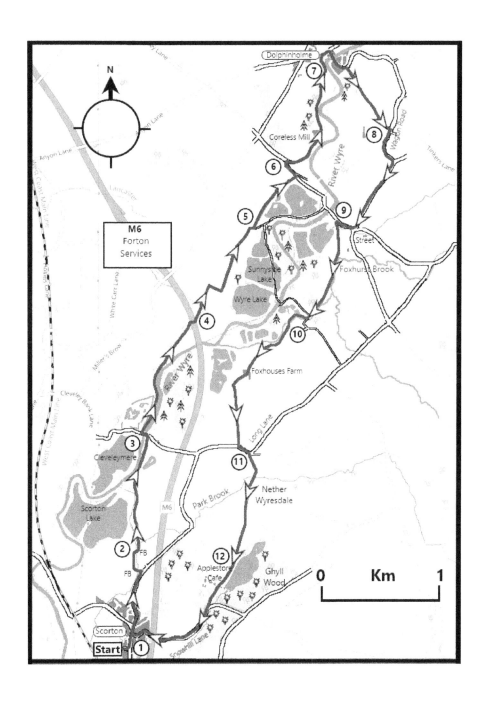

Walk Description

Starting from the pretty village of Scorton the route follows the Wyre Way on a well marked, delightful path following the course of the River Wye as it meanders through a maze of lakes with names like Sunnyside, Fox's, and Cleveley Mere. The path crosses many footbridges (including the M6, this does not spoil the otherwise quiet rural scenery) and a few stiles before reaching Coreless Mill and Dolphinholme. The peaceful mill town is set astride the river and was once a hive of activity.

The return route follows field paths and a minor road to the small hamlet of Street, then on past a holiday village at Foxhouses. From here the route follows tracks which leads you on through Wyresdale, at the foot of Nicky Nook at 215 Mts. This marks the western edge of the Bleasdale Moor. The track enters woodland and is followed alongside Wyresdale Lake where the Applestore café in a peaceful woodland setting is a good place for a break. The final leg is along a quiet road leading on to the centre of Scorton.

Walk Directions

1. Turn left at the entrance to the car park, follow the road straight on out of the village. Turn left onto a waymarked path and across a footbridge, continue alongside the brook, cross another footbridge and follow the path to reach a track.

2. Follow the track past Scorton Lake and join another track alongside the River Wyre. Follow the track to a tarmac road.

3. Turn left across the bridge then turn right onto a path on the opposite bank of the river. The path passes through a wooded area between the river and fishing lodges before emerging onto a field path and a footbridge over the M6.

4. Cross the M6 and bear right from the steps follow a field path to a boundary hedge. Continue alongside the hedge to reach a track. Turn right then in a few Mt's, left through the grounds of Guy's Activity Centre. Cross a field path bearing right towards the right boundary hedge and look out for a footbridge, cross and bear left in a chalet park, continue through the park towards the entrance

5. Follow the drive to a small woodland at the entrance and look out for a path alongside the wood, turn left to follow the path, crossing a track then keep left alongside a hedge and pass a Fox's Lake on your right. Continue straight on to a ladder stile onto a road.

Fox's Lake

6. Turn left, follow the road 100Mts and turn right through a gate onto a track. Follow the track to Coreless Mill. Carry on, follow the field path and alongside a woodland boundary on your left. The path emerges onto a track, follow on around a terrace of mill cottages to reach a road bridge in Dolphinholme.

Mill cottages at Dolphinholme

7. Turn right, follow the road over the bridge on the River Wyre, at a sharp left bend, turn right off the road onto a waymarked path through a wood. Follow the path out of the wood uphill passing an old stone chimney, cross a couple of fields and stiles, continue along a wooded field boundary then cross a footbridge, bear left across another field to reach Wagon Road.

8. Turn right, follow the road, turn right at a T junction and follow the road to a crossroads at Street. Turn right, follow the road 100Mts. And turn left at a waymarked path through a gate at a car park.

9. From the small car park bear left across a field path, follow the path alongside a woodland and Foxhouse Brook.
The path skirts right around and crosses an access road to holiday chalets.

10. Continue on alongside the woodland then cross a footbridge to follow a field boundary hedge to reach Foxhouses Farm. Pass through the farmyard and follow the access track to the entrance on Long Lane.

11. Turn left, follow the road a few Mts. then turn right onto a minor road, keep following the road which enters woodland and becomes narrower. At a sharp left bend, continue straight ahead over a cattle grid on a track. The track passes Applestore café on your right and Wyresdale Lake left.

12. From the car park at Applestore café continue on to reach the tarmacked Snowhill Lane. Follow the road straight ahead, which crosses over the M6 back to Scorton. At the T junction, turn left for The Barn car park.

Historical notes on Dolphinholme

The unusual name of the village derives from an ancient Scandinavian settlement and has nothing to do with the marine mammal! In 1784 the first mechanised worsted spinning mill was established here, and a factory village grew up around this early industrial site. That mill closed in 1865, but another, Coreless Mill, continued working until 1926.The route we follow passes the mill, before reaching its heyday it employed upwards of a thousand wool spinners, wool combing was carried out in every home. These 18th-century stone cottages were built for workers at the nearby mill, which was originally water-driven - its wheel was second only in size to that of Laxey on the Isle of Man. In 1811, the village and factory were amongst the first to be lit by gas, and in 1822 the mill was converted to steam. The yarn was transported to Leeds and Bradford for weaving.

Coreless Mill

WALK 17
Grizedale and Nicky Nook

A woodland walk through Grizedale and Holme Wood, followed by the magnificent view point of Nicky Nook.

ROUTE SUMMARY	Wyresdale Park – Grizedale – Holme Wood – Fell End – Nicky Nook
START	Applestore Cafe

LOCATION & ATTRIBUTES	
Distance and Grading	5 ½ Miles 1000 Feet (305 Mt's) ascent moderate *Alternative Route A* 5 Miles 738 Feet (225 Mt's) ascent easy
Route conditions	Mostly level well marked paths with one steep stretch. May be rough and muddy in places. Quite a few stiles and some quiet roadside walking. *Alternative Low Level Route avoids the steep stretch over Nicky Nook*
Postcode	PR3 1BA
Grid Reference	SD 509492
Refreshments	The Applestore at Wyresdale
Car parking	Car park at the Applestore cafe
Toilets	As above

Directions to the walk

Leave the M6 at junction 33, take first exit at a roundabout, follow the A6 towards Preston. After 3 miles past an Esso garage turn left onto

Station Lane, follow over a narrow bridge to Scorton Village, turn right at crossroads then left at Stouts Bar. Follow the road to a crossroads with Applestore café signed straight ahead. The car park is 150 yards ahead on the track

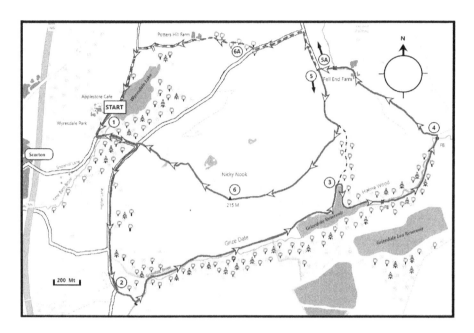

Walk Description

Starting from the popular Applestore Café, the walk quickly reaches the woodland of Grizedale and follows the course of Grizedale Brook. Exceptionally beautiful in spring with many wild flowers, including bluebells. The sounds of birdsong and babbling water accompany you all the way to Grizedale Reservoir. From here, the route continues to follow a permissive path through more delightful woodland some stretches are on boardwalks and footbridges through Holme Wood before emerging at the foot of the Bleasdale Fells.

The route continues on past Fell End Farm named after Harrisend Fell.From here, either over Nicky Nook which involves a fairly steep (but rewarding) climb or around the hill via Potters Hill Farm.

The Nicky Nook route takes you up to the trig point where the views over Morecambe Bay open up, a great place for a breather before the finale. The path slowly descends before a final steep stretch back onto the lane which returns you to Scorton and the well-earned refreshments which are to be had at the Applestore cafe. The low level route follows a lane and a woodland path to Potters Hill Farm, from here it is a short level walk on a country lane back to the Applestore Café.

Walk Directions

1. From the car park follow the track back to Snowhill Lane and turn left. Follow the road up hill to a T junction on Higher Lane and turn right, follow the road 800 Mt's to a waymarker and gate on the left.

2. Pass through, and follow a field path to a stile and gate next to a footbridge over Grizedale Brook, turn left to follow the broad brookside path. Eventually the path passes alongside the reservoir and steps leading up to Nicky Nook on your left. Ignore these. Carry straight on the path as it turns left round an inlet of the reservoir.

The path through Holme Wood

3. At the end of the inlet, look out for a gate onto a path on your right, pass through and follow the path through Holme Wood and alongside the head of the reservoir. The path becomes narrow and follows the brook through dense woodland which is a delight with woodland flowers and birdsong. A stretch is on boardwalks and over footbridges.

4. Following a footbridge climb the path out of the wood up to a T junction of paths and turn left. Follow the path alongside a wall then across two fields and gates to reach a track, continue ahead through agate to Fell Foot Farm. Pass between buildings, bear left through the farm, follow the entry track to the tarmacked road

From here a there is a choice of high and low routes, the route over Nicky Nook follows on from Point 5. The low route from 5A.

5. Turn left, follow the track. Bear right at a fork passing a Reservoir building on the right. The path ascends steeply from here past a stone pillar, continue on across a wall stile and visit the Trig Point pillar. Stop and soak up the view!

The view from the Trig pillar on Nicky Nook

6. From the trig point follow the broad path bearing right steadily downhill, passing a tarn on your right then another smaller one on the left. The path is quite steep here, follow down to reach a stile onto Higher Lane. Opposite is Snowhill Lane, continue on the lane to return to the car park on the right at the Applestore café.

The Low Level Route

5A. Turn right, follow the road to a junction and turn left, follow this road which enters a wooded area, look out for a stile on the right.

6A. Cross and follow the faint path through woodland, bearing left and continue along a line of trees to a gate. Pass through onto a farm track at Potters Hill Farm. Pass the farm buildings onto the entrance track and follow straight on to reach a crossway. Turn left and follow the track which brings you back to the car park at the Applestore café

WALK 18

Abbeystead and the Wyre Way

This outstanding walk follows the Wyre Way past the spectacular weir and on towards Dolphinholme, then returning up the beautiful valley to the headwaters at Tarnbrook where the Wyre Way brings you back to Abbeystead

ROUTE SUMMARY	Abbeystead – Lentworth Hall – Lee – Tarnbrook – Tower Lodge - Marshaw
START	Abbeystead, Stoops Bridge car park
LOCATION & ATTRIBUTES	
Distance and Grading Shortened Route	9 Miles 879 Feet (270 Mts.) ascent Hard 4 Miles 337 Feet(103 Mts.)ascent Easy
Route conditions	Mainly level paths, with a few stiles The full route has a fairly long steep stretch. Some pleasant, quiet lane walkingS
Postcode	LA2 9BQ
Grid Reference	SD 563543
Refreshments	A packed lunch is required
Car parking	Stoops Bridge Public car park off Strait Lane
Toilets	No facilities on the route

Directions to the walk

Leave the M6 at junction 33, follow the A 6 toward Preston, in 100 Mt's turn left onto minor road for Abbeystead, after half Km. turn left againand left at another junction onto Anyon Lane, follow the signs for Abbeystead. At Dolphinholme cross a double mini roundabout bearing right at the signed Abbeystead Road. Follow for 3 ½ Miles. The car park is on your right at the Stoops road bridge

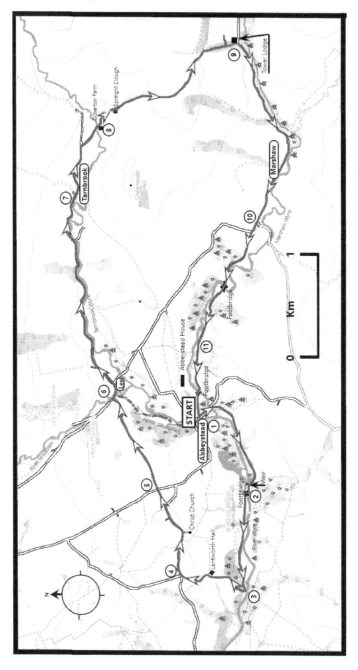

Walk Description

Abbeystead nestles in a valley formed by the Rivers Tarnbrook, Wyre and Marshaw Wyre which join at Abbeystead to form the River Wyre. The rivers drain the western hills of Forest of Bowland. The walk starts here and follows a riverside path through woodland towards Dolphinholme. The River Wyre is crossed after passing the spectacular

weir before the valve house

The weir at Abbeystead

and site a disaster that occurred in 1984. Sixteen visitors attending the opening of a new pump system were killed in an explosion. A plaque can be seen in memory to those who lost their lives.

The route continues alongside the river in beautiful quiet countryside before leaving the Wyre Way up past Lentworth Hall and the isolated church of Christ Church with a nice view over the rolling hills which are with you for much of the route. The walk follows field paths crossing stiles and brooks before reaching the tiny settlement at Lee where the shortened route can be followed to return to Stoops Bridge. The full route continues on a long track alongside the Tarnbook Wyre upstream past farms towards Tarnbrook.

The scenery changes to bare open moorland ahead as you progress up the valley towards the hills of Brennand. Curlews may be seen and heard circling overhead with their mournful piping. Other moorland birds such as Wheatears and Pippets are to be seen. Following the farming hamlet at Tarnbrook, the route climbs over a short stretch of the moorland to reach the high point of the walk at c 280 Mts. before descending down into the valley of the River Marshaw Wyre.

The Wyre Way continues along a delightful stretch of road alongside the river as it flows down past Marshaw. From here the river is followed on field paths. and a crossing on a footbridge before continuing alongside the looping river. The grounds of Abbeystead House, the Duke of Westminster's family residence, will be seen with its pristine gardens, before a bridge is crossed a short distance before you reach. the car park.

The route follows a mixture of field paths, quiet lanes and tracks. Be prepared for some muddy conditions and a few stiles. There are a couple of short steep stretches but not too taxing. The walk is an absolute joy in fine weather in spring or summer, but is good at all times of the year in reasonable weather.

Walk Directions

1. Turn right from the car park cross over Marshaw Wyre then turn off the road right to follow a path through Hinberry Wood. Keep straight on at a junction and follow the path alongside the River Wyre. The path emerges alongside the spectacular weir on the Abbeystead Reservoir.

2. Cross the footbridge after the weir and turn left past the pump house chamber and memorial. Follow the track and shortly onto a path parallel to the river, rejoin the track and follow to a gate.

3. Shortly after passing through the gate turn right uphill to reach the large farmstead at Lentworth Hall pass between the buildings to the access drive and follow up to a crossroads.

4. Turn right, follow the road, continue on past the entrance to Christ Church, look out for a gate on the left with a waymarked field path parallel to the road, cross the field to another road.

5. Cross the stile onto the lane then pass through the gate opposite and follow the track then a path along a left field boundary. Pass through a gate and continue along the right hand boundary. Over a stile and steep bank. Continue on the field path before dropping steeply down to a

Grizedale Bridge

wall stile onto a road. Cross the wall stile and turn right , the full route continues to follow the road over the River Grizedale.

.

The shortened route is through a gate immediately before the bridge onto a track, follow the track which brings you alongside the Tarnbrook Wyre and leads on to Stoops Bridge.

6. Turn left at a junction, follow the narrow road up the valley to Tarnbrook. The road follows the course of the Tarnbrook Wyre.

7. At Tarnbrook the route is joined by the Wyre Way which is followed from here on to return to Abbeystead. Go straight on up to the fellside, bear right at a fork to drop down to cross the river at Gilberton Farm.

8. Bear left from the farm and pass over a stream and through a gate. Continue on uphill passing through a gate at Spreight Clough, follow the path alongside a wall. Cross a couple of wallstiles, after passing asheepfold at the top of Hind Hill, bear left through a gate. Cross a couple of fields diagonally to join a track at a fingerpost. Turn right down the track to reach Tower Lodge.

9. Turn right, follow the road alongside Marshaw Wyre passing the Marshaw Farm on the right to a road junction.

10. Carry on straight ahead past the junction, then leave the road at a right hand bend, Pass through a waymarked gate for the Wye Way and follow the path straight ahead. Cross a footbridge the bridge and bear left to follow the riverside path.

Footbridge on the Wyre Way near Abbeystead

11. At a fork keep straight on, the grounds of Abbeystead House may be seen on your right across the river. Cross a footbridge, cross a field path to reach the lane and car park at Stoops Bridge.

WALK 19

Glasson Dock and Cockersand Abbey

A walk with open views over the Lune estuary , a visit to the remote ruins of Cockersand Abbey, followed by a pleasant stroll along the Lancaster Canal

ROUTE SUMMARY	Glasson – River Lune – Cockersand Abbey – Upper Thurnham – Lancaster Canal
START	Glasson Dock car park
LOCATION & ATTRIBUTES	
Distance and Grading	9 Miles 370Feet (113 Mt's) ascent moderate (May be shortened to 8 miles)
Route conditions	Level with few stiles, a couple of field paths and some roadside walking.
Postcode	LA2 0BS
Grid Reference	SD 446561
Refreshments	A choice of pubs and cafes at Glasson Dock
Car parking	Car park at Glasson Dock
Toilets	As above

Directions to the walk

Leave the M6 at junction 33, follow the A6 towards Galgate. Turn left at traffic lights on the crossroads in Galgate ,then shortly after, bear left onto a minor road signed Conder Green. At Conder Green bear left at a fork then turn left onto the A588, cross a bridge then turn rightonto the B5290 for Glasson Dock. The car park is on the right at the dock.

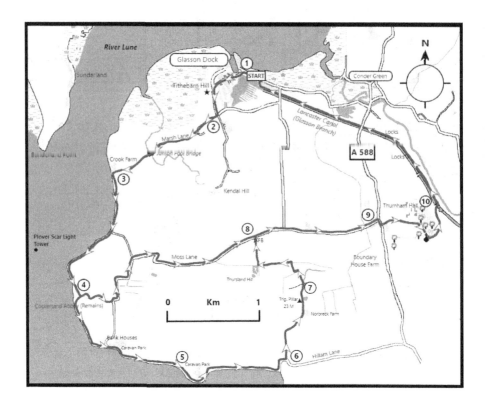

Walk Description

The start of the walk is by crossing the connecting lock between the dock and the Lancaster Canal terminus marina before reaching the coastal path on the Lune estuary. A limited amount of commercial shipping still uses the dock, with outbound shipments including coal, and incoming cargoes including animal foodstuffs and fertilizer.

The route follows the path over Tithebarn Hill where the views open up over the Lune estuary and the vast Morecambe Bay towards Sunderland Point and Heysham Power Station. The coastal path and track are followed and soon after rounding a point at Plover Hill, the route passes the site of Cockersand Abbey, built as a hospital in 1184. The abbey was dissolved in 1539 and the only significant relic that remains intact is a vaulted chapter house which was built in 1230 and used as a family mausoleum by the Daltons of Thurnham Hall during the 18th and 19th centuries.

The route continues to follow the coastal path and a track across a dyke before turning inland to pass the small hillock marked by a trig point at Norbreck Farm .From here paths follow field paths and drainage channels and a lane to reach Upper Thurnham and Thurnham Hall, a stone built 17th century house built for Robert Dalton, now used as a resort hotel. The church of St Thomas and St Elizabeth also partly funded by the Daltons, stands a little further on. The large ornate Lych Gate is passed before turning off the road onto field paths which lead you to the bank of the Glasson Branch of the Lancaster Canal for a pleasant 1 ½ mile walk to return to Glasson Dock.

Walk Directions

1. From the car park follow the road over the bridge at the dock entrance to the marina,
At a T road junction where there is a grand vista over the Lune estuary turn left . Follow the road then turn right onto Marsh Lane.

2. Follow the lane which becomes a track, pass a caravan site and through a couple of gates,

Janson Pool Bridge

cross Janson Pool bridge to reach a Crook Farm,
bear left to follow the track alongside the estuary.

3. Follow the sea wall to reach a remote house at a junction. Continue to follow the sea wall. The light tower on the Plover Scar rocks bridge becomes prominent
offshore as you proceed to the remains of Cockersand Abbey.

4. Bear left to view the ruins. (*From here the route may be shortened by continuing on through a gate onto a farm track, passing the front of the* *farm and crossing a stile and gate onto a lane(Moss Lane). Follow the lane, bear right at a junction, continue on for a mile to point 8.)*

The track on the sea defence dyke

The full route continues along the coastal path to Bank Houses, passing a derelict observation house . Follow the path around the Bank Houses caravan park. Continue on to a fence boundary.

5. Pass through a boundary gate and continue along the road around a headland on the path follow onto a sea defence dyke . Cross the dyke to a track junction

6. Turn left to follow the track as it bends right ,then turn off onto the track for Norbreck Farm .Follow the track to the farm .Bear left at a fork and turn left onto a track .As it bends left carry straight on to the trig pillar next to a pond. This is the highest spot at 23 Mts for miles around . Carry on bearing right to return to the track.

7. At the field boundary hedge pass through a gate and bear left leaving the track ,follow the field path straight on pass around the head of a ditch to reach a stile on the field boundary opposite. Cross and turn left to follow the field boundary hedge to a path junction near a fishing lake Turn right, follow the path to a footbridge onto Moss Lane.

8. Turn right, *(the shortened route continues straight on)* follow the lane, carry straight on at a the junction with Jeremy Lane for Thurnham. Pass farms and cottages to reach a road junction with the A588.

9. Turn right , follow the road a few yards to the entrance to Thurnham Hall ,turn left to follow the drive . Keep straight on past the car park for the hall, bearing right to reach the impressive Lych Gate for St Thomas and St. Elizabeth Church. Turn left, crossing a stile at a gate onto a path alongside a wood, follow the path which brings you to the locks on the Glasson Branch of the Lancaster Canal.

The lych gate at St Thomas and St Elizabeth church

10. Cross the bridge at the locks and turn to pass under the bridge onto the towpath, passing a jetty on the canal , follow the path for a pleasant 1½ mile stroll to return to Glasson Dock.

Lock on the Glasson Branch of Lancaster Canal

WALK 20
Lancaster Waterway Walk

The walk follows the Lancaster Canal as it wends its way through the historical city. Returning on the bank of the Lune along the city waterfront.

ROUTE SUMMARY	Lune Aqueduct – Lancaster Canal – Aldcliffe – Lancashire Coastal Way - St George's Quay – Riverside Park
START	Aqueduct car park on Caton Road(A589)
LOCATION & ATTRIBUTES	
Distance and Grading	7 ½ Miles 287 Feet (88Mt's) ascent moderate
Route conditions	Level easy walking, one stile, mainly firm even walkways and no gradients except for the steps up to the canal
Postcode	LA1 3PE
Grid Reference	SD 487637
Refreshments	White Cross pub on the canal in the city centre and many others are close to the route in the city. Also, Macdonald's next the car park
Car parking	Aqueduct car park
Toilets	City centre pubs and cafes

Directions to the walk

Leave the M6 at J 34 ,turn onto A589 for Lancaster, the Aqueduct car park is 1 mile on the right

108

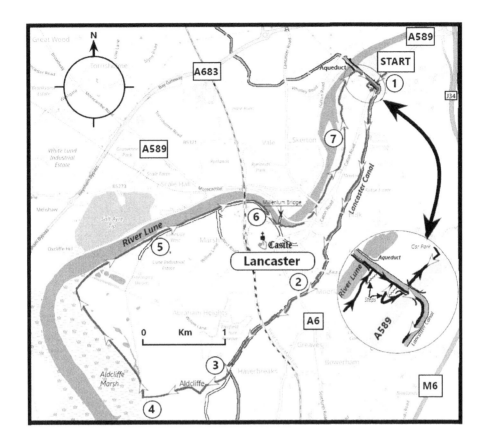

Walk Description

From the car park you ascend steps which lead up to the canal towpath, turn right to follow the Lancaster Canal for a leisurely walk into the city. At bridge 100 the cathedral may be seen, soon after ,a ramp leads onto a bridge and the route crosses to the opposite bank. The White Cross pub is passed and further along the Water Witch pub with its canal side tables.

The canal in this area has basins with quays and warehouses . It is full of character and evocative of the days when this was a hive of activity. Soon after, the canal is crossed again on a stone bridge ,and the route turns back under the bridge, to continue on the canal towpath which runs parallel to a minor road and soon after, passes under the west coast main line railway bridge.

The canal towpath is left to pass on old Lodge House for Aldcliffe Hall, where there is a big change in the landscape with flat open farmland around the village of Aldcliffe. A lane takes you through the village and onto a path across the pastures to the River Lune. A footpath leads you along the foreshore of the tidal marshlands with views of the river and bird life. Wading birds such as Redshank, Egrets and Herons as well as Lapwing and Oyster Catchers may be seen.

The Millennium Bridge

The path merges onto a riverside road to reach the centre of Lancaster's attractions, including the Millennium bridge. The route follows part of the bridge then on to pass under the Greyhound Bridge which once carried the railway to Morecombe and Heysham from Lancaster Green Ayre Station.

The line from here was electrified as early as 1908 using overhead lines. In 1953, it was used as a test bed for the electrification of the West Coast Main Line and closed following the infamous Beeching report in 1966 .

The route continues to follow the riverside on the trackbed of the railway from the site of Green Ayre Station to Wennington and Skipton. Eventually the imposing structure of the Lune Aqueduct comes into view. Climb the steps to view the aqueduct from the towpath and cross over the river to admire the scenery and the masonry in its construction .It was built by John Rennie and completed in 1797. Return by descending the steps used at the start of the walk next to the road bridge over the A589, turn to pass under the canal to the car park.

Walk directions

1. Turn right at the entrance ,pass under the canal then climb the steps to reach the towpath and turn right, the opposite bank has open green fields and woodland , until Dolphinlee Bridge where the canal enters residential areas. The canal is a green corridor through the urban areas of Lancaster where ducks and swans have made their home. Lancaster Cathedral comes into view at Moor Lane Bridge. After passing the cathedral the towpath crosses to the opposite bank at Quarry Road bridge

Lancaster Canal near Moor Lane Bridge

.

2. Pass under Quarry Road then turn right up to the footbridge alongside the road ,cross the canal and descend to the opposite bank and continue along the towpath. The towpath passes the White Cross pub restaurant and further along the Water Witch pub restaurant , the starting point for canal cruises and where the warehouses , basins and quays can be seen opposite. The pub is a chance maybe for a quick break before continuing on to the remoter part of the walk. Shortly the pub the towpath reverts back to the opposite bank by crossing the Aldcliffe Yard road bridge. Turn down the spiral path right ,onto the opposite bank to pass under the bridge and continue.on the towpath. Pass under the West Coast Main Railway Line and follow the canal to a left hand bend.

3. Leave the canal towpath to pass through the gateway at the Lodge onto Aldcliffe Drive ,follow the tree lined drive into the pretty village. Turn right at a T junction ,follow the road straight out of the village to a

The path along the dyke on the River Lune

gate and stile at a sharp right turn. This is the site of the level crossing on the dismantled railway between Lancaster and Glasson Dock.

4. Cross the stile and turn right to follow the flood defensive dyke alongside the River Lune. The path is part of the Lancashire Coastal Way. Continue to follow around a right bend to a path junction turn left and continue to follow the riverside path. At a fork bear left , continue to follow the path to reach New Quay Road and continue alongside the river.

The crooked House on St George's Quay

5. Pass under the railway bridge where Lancaster Priory can be seen above Quay Meadows. Look out for the fantastic crooked house next to the George and Dragon Pub on St George's Quay.

6. From the quay, bear left to cross the Millennium Bridge. do not cross the river, rather at a T junction turn right to keep to the south bank of the river. The path curves to pass under the Greyhound Bridge Road, this bridge once carried the railway line to Morecambe and Heysham

Continue along the river bank through a small park ,once the site of Green Ayre railway station . From here on to the Lune Aqueduct the route follows the dismantled railway line. There is a plaque ,information board and a railway crane marking the site. Pass through an arched bridge with its railway number still remaining on its stonework.

7. Continue to follow the broad track, part of the "Lune Valley Ramble" towards Kirkby Lonsdale. Skerton Weir is passed before the Lune Viaduct

The Lune Aqueduct from the Lune Valley Ramble path

comes into sight.

Climb the steps to reach the towpath ,turn left to take in the views from this impressive monument to the canal age,before turning about to return to the steps leading down to Caton Road. Turn left on the road, pass under the canal to return to the car park.

WALK 21

Crossgill and Littledale

A walk in a remote dale nestled in the northern flank of the Bowland fells, following paths where peace and tranquillity are guaranteed.

ROUTE SUMMARY	The Cragg – Crossgill – Littledale Hall – Foxdale – Udale – Skelbow Barn
START	Layby on Littledale Road at The Cragg
LOCATION & ATTRIBUTES	
Distance and Grading	5 ½ Miles 735Feet (224Mt's) ascent moderate
Route conditions	Paths can be rough and muddy in places. Mostly level with a few short steep stretches and a couple of stiles.
Postcode	LA2 9ET
Grid Reference	SD 545618
Refreshments	None on route
Car parking	At a layby at the Cragg on Littledale Road
Toilets	None on route

Directions to the walk

Leave the M6 at junction 34, follow the A683 towards Kirkby Lonsdale. Turn right at Caton onto road marked. Quernmore. After 2 ½ miles bear left at a fork for Quernmore onto Postern Gate Road. At a crossroads turn left for Littledale, after 2 ½ miles park on a layby with an information board at The Cragg (just before a cattle grid).

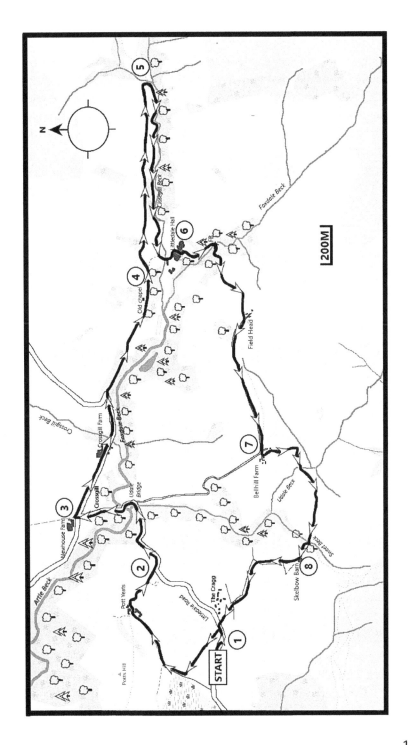

115

Walk Description

A great walk a little off the beaten track, lovely in spring with an abundance of birdlife wild flowers and daffodils alongside the quiet roads. Great views of the Bowland fells and a varied landscape with woodlands, moorland and a delightful brookside walk up Littledale.

Starting at a lay by on Littledale Road which winds north of Clougha Pike, the walk set off across moorland which is the home of nesting Lapwings. A track is followed past isolated farms before dropping down to the bridges crossing the Udale and Artle Becks at the tiny hamlet of Crossgill. A scout camp site is sited here, an ideal spot to experience the best of the Lancashire countryside.

Moving on, the route follow a very quiet lane with daffodils lining both sides in spring. There are some lovely houses dotted along the lane including the Old Church House. Soon after passing the entrance to Littledale Hall, a farmtrack leads on through woodland where an old enigmatic chapel stands. By the look of the interior, it is home to many nesting birds! It must have meant quite a walk for its congregation being so far away from habitation.

The route carries on to reach another change of scenery as the views open up above the Closegill Beck near Littledale Hall. A path is followed up the narrowing dale contouring the hillside above the dale and crossing the occasional brook until dropping down to follow Closegill Beck downstream back to Littledale Hall.

The large complex of buildings around the impressive hall are passed at the bridge over the brook before following a woodland path up Foxdale then crossing Foxdale Beck on a footbridge. Here there is a steep but thankfully short stretch through woodland before crossing pastureland with great views over the Fells and Foxdale.

A track leads on past a couple more farms before the route drops down to cross the Udale and well named Sweet Becks. A small climb brings you up to pass Skelbow barn then the home stretch gently uphill to return to Littledale Road at The Cragg.

Walk directions

1. Walk up hill right to the cattle grid, cross the grid then turn sharp left at the fingerpost, onto a marsh grassy field path. Head for a gnarled

116

tree against a stone wall. Turn right here ,don't cross the stile(the path ahead is usually flooded!)Follow the stone wall up to the farm track. Turn right, follow the track to the farmstead at Pott Yeats. Pass between the farm buildings bearing right past the last one to continue along the track.

2. Follow the track to another farm building and a junction with Littledale Road, turn left, follow the road and cross a bridge over Udale Beck, turn left at a road junction and cross Foxdale Beck. Pass a scout camp and continue uphill to a crossroads at New House Farm and turn right . This road is lined with daffodils in spring.

3. Continue along the road passing the entrance to Littledale Hall, at a sharp left bend carry straight onto the waymarked track through a gate, follow the track passing an abandoned chapel on your left, continue to follow the track ahead.

The derelict chapel at Littledale

4. Bear left onto a path at a fork and contour around a defile , passing over brooks. Continue to follow the track which becomes a path. Cross a footbridge over a brook ,continue to contour the valley upstream to reach a wall crossing the valley with a wall stile and a farmtrack crossing a ford

5. Drop down right to join the track alongside Closegill Beck (don't cross the wall stile). Turn right to follow the track to reach the farm at Littledale Hall. At a track junction bear left to cross the beck and continue left through the farm yard.

The track and beck at Littledale Farm

6. Look out for a signed path at a gate on the right and turn to follow to a footbridge over Foxdale Beck. Cross and follow the steep winding path up out of the woodland and onto a field path alongside a boundary on your right. Pass through a gate onto a track and follow right to skirt round the farm and reach the access track then turn right . Follow the track to Belhill Farm.

7. Turn left through the farmyard and pass through a gate then follow the track alongside a boundary downhill. Follow the track right and cross a footbridge over Udale Beck at a ford, bear right to continue on the track to reach a line of trees, drop down to cross a footbridge over Sweet Beck then bear right to Skelbow Barn.

8. Pass through a gate on the right then bear right to follow the track uphill alongside a wall to your left. Pass through another gate and continue to follow the wall on your right to reach a ladder stile and gate, cross and turn left to the lay by on Littledale Road.

The gate and stile at The Cragg on Littledale Road

WALK 22
Hest Bank Coast and Canal Walk

A walk of two half's, first half follows the Lancashire Coastal Way with grand views over the Morecambe Bay. The second follows a scenic stretch of the Lancaster Canal

ROUTE SUMMARY	Hest Bank – Wild Duck Hall – River Keer – Crag Bank – Lancaster Canal – Bolton le Sands
START	Hest Bank car park
LOCATION & ATTRIBUTES	
Distance and Grading	7 Miles 400Feet (122 Mt's) ascent moderate
Route conditions	Level with a few stiles, and field paths some quiet roadside walking. Good boots required for the boggy conditions on the salt marsh.
Postcode	LA2 6HN
Grid Reference	SD 468666
Refreshments	The Shore Café at the car park, and The Bay Crossing near the level crossing.
Car parking	Car park at Hest Bank
Toilets	As above

Directions to the walk

Leave the M6 at junction 34, follow the A683 from the roundabout towards Morecambe. Take the second exit at the next roundabout for the A6 signed Carnforth. Turn left onto Hest Bank Lane at the "Slyne with Hest" signs. Follow the road through the village, and over the canal bridge, then take the first right onto Station Road, follow down to cross the A5105 and the level crossing to reach The Shore car park.

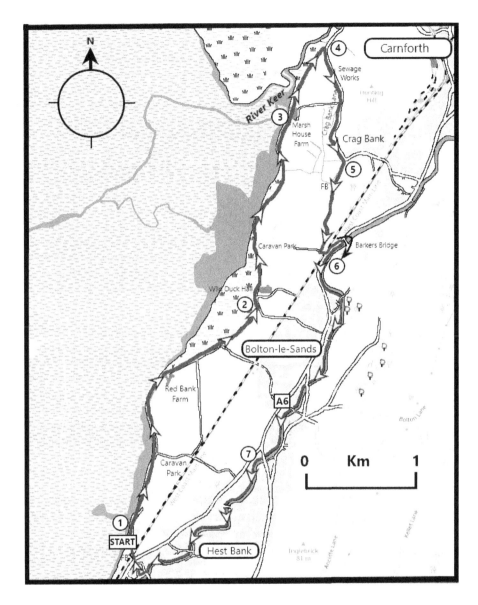

Walk Description

This is a level walk with great views over the marshlands of Morecambe Bay with sea birds and a backdrop of Silverdale and the southern fells of the Lake District. Hest Bank is derived from the Old English 'haest' meaning

The car park at The Shore viewed from the

undergrowth while Slyne is from a word meaning slope. Neither of which can be seen now. The shore is bordered by salt marsh with a mosaic of tidal

channels and pools which are only covered at spring high tides. A great place for spotting wild fowl and wading birds probing the muddy channels.

The start follows part of Lancashire Coastal Way, a 137-mile walk, the path is a little hard to follow in places but if you keep close to the shore you won't go far wrong. The second half of the walk follows a field paths and a "green lane" to reach the towpath of the very scenic Lancaster Canal. The canal has no locks making the going easy on the level hard surface. Many private gardens can be viewed on the opposite bank making for a very pleasurable walk all the way back to Hest Bank.

Walk directions

1. Follow the track from the car park to the path along the shore, at a caravan park at Red Bank Farm, follow the path on an embankment then onto a track leading to a lane. Continue to follow this left and left again

The shoreline at Red Bank Farm

to pass around the evocatively named Wild Duck Hall, a large restored property.

2. Just beyond the hall leave the track to follow a faint path below a large caravan park across the marshes, which can be a bit tricky, you have to pick your way through to avoid the muddier spots, but not a problem when wearing good boots. The path improves at the Black Dike Outfall and becomes a track which can be followed on the perimeter of the shore past Marsh House Farm.

3. The track follows the bank of the River Keer, beyond the river, Warton Crag is prominent ,and a track circuit for trail bikes which at times can get noisy. The track ends at a gate and stile leading onto a lane. (Crag Bank Lane).

4. Turn right and follow the lane past the sewage works and carry on to reach a residential area and a sharp left bend.

5. Turn right at a waymarker, cross a stile next a gate onto a track, cross another stile left of a gate and continue ahead alongside a ditch on your right. Cross a footbridge, continue alongside a ditch, cross another stile and follow the track which climbs to another stile beside a gate.

This gives access to a delightful hedged "green way" to reach a tarmac road. Turn left, cross the railway bridge onto the A6.

6. Turn left, follow the road 150 Mt's, cross the road carefully to a layby and access road to Barkers Bridge over the Lancaster Canal. Swing sharp right onto the canal towpath before the bridge. Continue to follow the towpath to pass through Bolton le Sands. After bridge 124 The Royal pub can be accessed by steps down from the towpath should you care for a refreshment break.

A swing bridge on the Lancaster Canal

7. The towpath passes under the A6 and continues along a very winding stretch of the canal with many beautiful gardens on the opposite bank.A swing bridge is passed before reaching bridge No 118, climb the ramped path to leave the tow path onto the road over the bridge, carry straight on a 100 Mt's and turn right down Station Road. Follow the road to the A5105, cross to reach The Shore car park.

WALK 23
Arkholme and the Lune Valley

This walk passes through the Lune Valley, a peaceful rural landscape between the timeless hamlets of Arkholme, Gressingham and Eskrigge.

ROUTE SUMMARY	Arkholme – Gressingham – Eskrigge – The Snab-River Lune – Loyn Bridge – Lune Valley Ramble Path
START	Arkholme village hall car park
LOCATION & ATTRIBUTES	
Distance and Grading	7 ½ Miles 570Feet (174Mt's) ascent moderate
Route conditions	Paths are generally level; some field paths and a short stretch of riverside path can be muddy. A few stiles and some quiet roadside walking
Postcode	LA6 1AT
Grid Reference	SD 584723
Refreshments	Bay Horse Hotel Arkholme at the crossroads near the car park
Car parking	Village Hall car park
Toilets	Toilets at the Bay Horse Hotel

Directions to the walk

Leave the M6 at junction 35, follow the B6254 towards Kirkby Lonsdale. Arkholme is 4 ½ miles, the car park is 100 Mt's past the crossroads in the village centre.

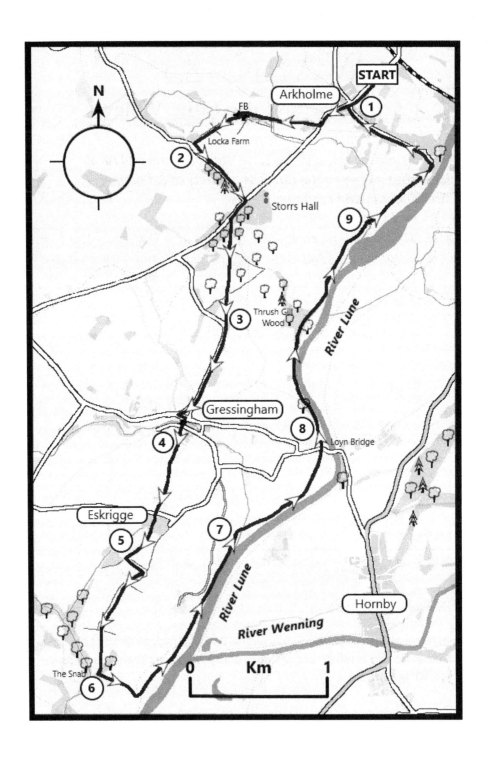

Walk Description

The route starts at Arkholme, which is a charming stone village dating from 17th and 18th century. The route crosses field paths past Storrs Hall which is hidden by trees, this is a Tudor gothic mansion built in 1848. Soon after the route enters Gressingham, the church has a fine doorway of Norman vintage. 'Gressingham Duck' is well known in restaurants all over the country this has been bred in the area by crossing Perkin (a common white duck) and wild Mallard resulting in a gamey tasting dish

Following on, the route climbs gently to reach a viewpoint at 85 Mts. giving panoramic views over the River Lune towards the Yorkshire Dales. From here the route drops down to "The Snab" where the Lune Valley Path is joined for a delightful riverside walk through a mixture of woodland and meadowland scenery. The path is 16 miles long from Lancaster to Kirby Lonsdale.

The Loyn Bridge marks the halfway point on the return path, it dates from 1684 and is the only crossing of the Lune between Caton and Kirby Lonsdale. It is designated an ancient monument and is overlooked by a Norman earthwork of Castle Cede. The route is completed by following the riverside path to reach Main Street at Arkholme

Walk directions

1. Turn left at entrance of village hall car park, continue straight on at the crossroads. Following a left hand bend cross a stile on the right and follow the wall of Bainsbeck House, pass through a farm gate and bear left. Cross a footbridge and a squeeze stile and bear left on another field path. Pass through a gate and follow the field path towards a bungalow on the right. Pass through a small gate, follow the garden path to a drive onto the Locka Lane.

2. Turn left to follow the road to a junction then turn right. Look out for an unmarked gap in the wall on your left. Turn through the gap and follow through a wood and carry straight on to follow a field path. Pass through agate and carry straight on. Cross a stile and continue in the same direction to reach a gate onto a road.

3. Turn left to follow the road to Gressingham, at a fork, bear right, in a few Mt's. at a T junction cross the road onto a track past a bench seat and cross a footbridge.

4. Turn left onto Eskrigge lane, follow for a few Mt's then turn right at the junction by a cottage. Follow the track, pass through a gate and follow the field paths straight across 3 fields. Cross a stile onto a track and cross Lea Lane to reach Eskrigge Farm. At Eskrigge House, pass through a gate on

Eskrigge Farm

the left then follow the field path along a boundary on your right.

5. After passing an isolated house, pass through a gate then turn left on a track uphill, follow right at the field boundary. Continue along the boundary hedge to reach a gap and gate, pass through, follow the right hand hedge to another gate and pass through onto a field path. Follow the crest of the hill with great views over the Lune Valley. Pass through a gate then bear left down to a farmhouse at Crow Wood.

6. Pass through a gate onto a track, follow on downhill. This is "The Snab". Turn off left sharply to pass through a gate, follow the path across a floodplain to the River Lune. Turn left at cattle feeding station to follow the

The gate and Waymarker at The Snab

riverside path upstream. passing the confluence of the River Wenning.

7. Cross a ford in woodland and continue on the riverside path to reach Loyn Bridge. Pass through a gate, cross the road turn left a few Mts. pass through another waymarked gate on the right. Continue to follow the riverside path.

8. Pass through woodland and cross a stile,.and a footbridge at Thrush Gill Wood. Continue along the riverside path.

9. Cross a small footbridge at a waymarker and continue to follow the river to reach a track, continue on the track to Main Street at Arkholme. Pass the John the Baptist church on your right and follow the road through the village to the crossroads, turn right at the Bay horse pub to reach the car park.

WALK 24

Leck Beck loop from Nether Burrow

A gentle pub walk on paths around the lower Leck Beck at its confluence with the River Lune.

ROUTE SUMMARY	Nether Burrow – Tunstall – Cowan Bridge – Over Burrow
START	Arkholme village hall car park
LOCATION & ATTRIBUTES	
Distance and Grading	5 ½ Miles 346Feet (106Mt's) ascent easy
Route conditions	Paths are generally level; some field paths and path can be muddy. A few stiles and some quiet roadside walking.
Postcode	LA6 2RJ
Grid Reference	SD 613752
Refreshments	The Highwayman at Nether Burrow
Car parking	As above
Toilets	As above

Directions to the walk

Leave the M6 at junction 34, follow the A683 towards Kirkby Lonsdale. Nether Burrow is about 9 miles, the Highwayman is on the right of the main road.

130

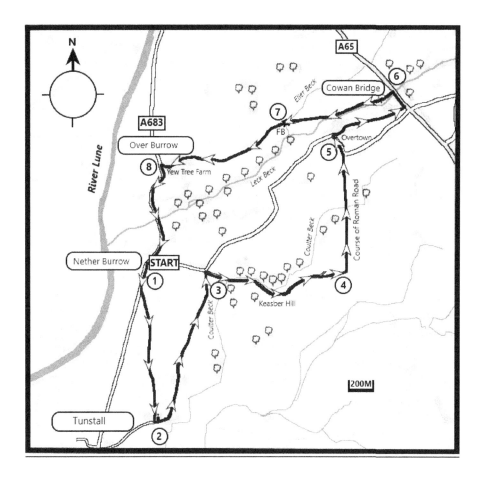

Walk Description

The walk crosses mainly flat fields at the foot of Barbon High Fell. This is the source of the waters of Leck Beck which drains west to join the River Lune at Nether Burrow. The area is famous for its pot holing, the landscape makes for an easy going any season walk, based at the wonderful Highwayman pub where hearty grub will be found, an ideal finish to the walk. The walk starts with a bridleway to the isolated church at Tunstall before following paths and tracks past farms and copses to reach a path following the line of a Roman Road typically straight as a die.

131

The path leads to Overtown and onto Cowan Bridge, where Leck Beck is crossed, shortly after a weir can be viewed,.. spectacular following heavy rain.

There follows a delightful path which follows the beck downstream, through beautiful quiet countryside all the way to Over Burrow. From here a short stretch of road leads back to The Highwayman where a great meal and drink awaits.

Walk directions

1. Leave the pub car park and turn left to follow the road. Pass through a gate on the left and follow the bridlepath. Cross two field boundaries, bear right at a fork keep right of the church ahead. Pass through the churchyard and squeeze stile and turn left on a minor road.

2. Turn left onto a track over a cattle grid and follow the track through the farmstead of Churchfield House. Pass Kirkriggs Barn. Marked on the OS map) and continue on to reach Woodman's Lane.

The copse on Keasber

3. Turn right and follow the waymarked track, cross a cattle grid and a prominent circular copse called Keasber Hill near Cowdber Farm.

4. At a stile and gate pass through and turn left to follow the path on the Roman Road alignment. At the end of the track carry straight onto the tarmacked road (Woodman Lane).

5. At a sharp left bend, turn right and follow straight on the track. The track ends at a private house, bear left then right to reach a stile and gate, cross and follow the path alongside a tall line of trees and across 3 fields to reach the main road.at Cowan Bridge Turn left on the main A65 road, keep left to follow the old road across the bridge over Leck Beck

6. Turn left after the bridge over Leck Beck and drop down to follow the riverside path passing the weir.Pass a private bridge over Leck Beck for Nethergayle. Continue on to reach a footbridge over Eller Beck.

The weir at Cowan Bridge

7. Continue on the path which follows the course of a small beck before joining a farm track past a barn then shortly after alongside a ford. The track passes through Yew Tree Farm, with pulley wheels decorating the walls. . Follow the track past the farm to the road and turn left.

8. Follow the road to past the entrance to Burrow Hall, cross the bridge over Leck Beck and return to the Highwayman.

WALK 25

Crooklands, Hincaster and the Lancaster Canal

The walk explores the long abandoned upper stretch of the Lancaster Canal including both portals of Hincaster Tunnel.

ROUTE SUMMARY	Crooklands – Lancaster Canal – Hincaster Tunnel – Hincaster – Woodhouse – Kidside - Milton
START	Crooklands Hotel car park

LOCATION & ATTRIBUTES	
Distance and Grading	6 ½ Miles 409 Feet (125 Mt's) ascent moderate
Route conditions	Mostly easy well marked paths, some road walking and numerous stiles. No steep slopes and some field paths which may be muddy in places
Postcode	LA7 7 NN
Grid Reference	SD 535836
Refreshments	The Crooklands Hotel
Car parking	Car park at the Crooklands Hotel. Also, on lay by on the B6385 over the canal bridge opposite the Hotel
Toilets	As above

Directions to the walk

Leave the M6 at junction 36, take first exit at a roundabout, follow the A65 towards Skipton. At the next roundabout take the first exit for Crooklands follow the road less than a mile, the Crooklands Hotel carpark is on the right. To park at the lay by, turn left on the B6385 over the canal bridge, the lay by is a few Mts. on the right.

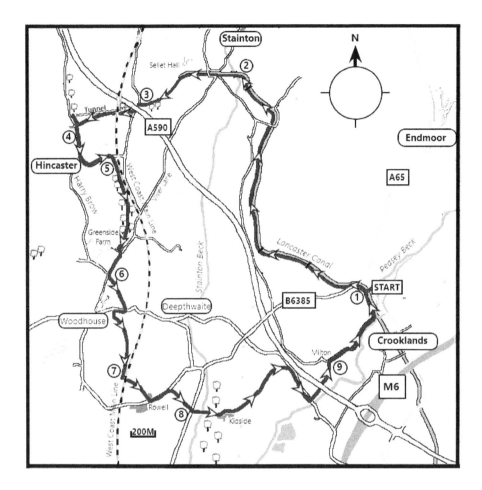

Walk Description

This walk is actually in Cumbria ,the border with Lancashire is a few miles south. The route starts at Crooklands, which is very conveniently a mile from the M6 Junction 36.The walk follows the truncated upper reaches of the disused Lancaster Canal. The easy level walk on the attractive grassy towpath passing under several bridges, wild fowl abounds with swans, moorhens, ducks and the occasional Heron. Stainton Beck is crossed on an aqueduct before reaching the end of the canal in water. Shortly after is the Hincaster Tunnel ,378 yards and built in 1817, it is driven through Tunnel Hill which is in fact a huge drumlin. The tunnel has no towpath and horses would have used a tunnel beneath the West Coast railway line. boats were hauled through the tunnel by way of a chain fixed to the wall. The route continues on a hedgerow lined path once used by the horses, a farm accommodation bridge neatly built for the height of the towpath horses, straddle the path.

Shortly after the west portal of the tunnel is visited before moving on to follow a minor road to the Hincaster Trailway which follows the route of a dismantled railway line from Hincaster to Arnside in South Cumbria the rails were lifted in1966. The route from here follows roads and field paths through peculiar drumlin landscape. (Thought to be created in the ice age by deposits of soft sediment from the melt waters.)

Quiet lanes are followed through the hamlets of Woodhouse and Rowton before crossing Stainton Beck at the farmstead of Kidside. from here a field path brings you to Milton and onto to the Lancaster Canal at Crooklands Aqueduct where Peasey Brook passes under the canal.The towpath is followed the short distance to return to the Crooklands Hotel.

Eastern portal on the dry Lancaster Canal

Walk Directions

1. From car park, cross the main road, follow the B 6385 opposite over the canal, turn right then join the canal towpath at a gap in the wall. Turn left to follow the towpath. Pass under four bridges before crossing an aqueduct over St.Sundays Beck.

Stainton Bridge

2. The next bridge 172 marks the end of the canal in water,   continue to follow the path along course of the now dry canal to reach a ramp down to a minor road.

3. Drop down to the road, turn left to pass under the A590, then turn right to return to the course of the canal. Soon after you reach the eastern portal of the Hincaster Tunnel, climb steps on the left, pass under the railway then bear right to follow a track once used by the towing horses to bypass the tunnel. Pass under a stone accommodation bridge built to fit a horse's dimensions on the track and continue.

The Accommodation Bridge at Hincaster

4. To see the western portal of the Hincaster Tunnel, turn right just before the   tarmacked road, follow the short track and return to the road. Turn left on the road (Harry Brow) passing a   drumlin on the right These are a feature of the local landscape. At a fork, bear left, follow the road to the next junction.

Carry straight on past a very grand house on the left. Keepstraight on towards a railway bridge then turn off the road on the right onto the Hincaster Trailway.

5. Follow the trail which passes through a wooded haven on the dismantled railway trackbed. At the trail end turn right onto Viver Lane and follow to the next junction.

6. Turn left onto the road signed Crooklands. The views from the road are a delight, with more round topped Drumlins on all sides. At a T junction turn right, follow for a few Mts. then turn left onto a track (unmarked at time of writing), follow the track bearing left. At a sharp right turn, carry straight onto a path alongside a boundary hedge, then cross into another field bearing right diagonally across the field towards the railway line. Follow the path alongside the railway to reach a track.

7. Turn left onto the track passing under the railway and between farm buildings then on through a farm at Rowell. At the tarmacked road (Rowell Lane) turn left. Follow the lane and look out for a waymarked gate on the right. Pass through and follow a field path diagonally left, aim for a solitary tree. Cross a stile in a hedge and cross the field path to another hedge.

8. Cross a stile onto the B6385, then follow the track opposite to Kidside. Cross the bridge over Stainton Beck and bear left at a fork at the farm then turn right off the track between farm buildings. Turn off the track to the left and cross a faint field path corner to corner, cross a stile and follow the hedge on the left through three fields to reach a stile on a tarmacked road. Turn right, follow the road to a gate and waymarked track on the left. Pass through and follow under the A590 to reach the hamlet of Milton.

9. At a T junction turn right, follow the lane, part of which runs alongside Peasey Beck to reach Crooklands Aqueduct. At a left hand bend climb the steps next the aqueduct to the canal towpath and turn left. Follow the towpath to return to the road bridge at Crooklands. Cross the bridge to return to the Crooklands Hotel.